Bengali (Bangla)

Dictionary & Phrasebook

Bengali (Bangla)

Dictionary & Phrasebook

Hanne-Ruth Thompson

Hippocrene Books
New York

For information, address:
HIPPOCRENE BOOKS, INC.
171 Madison Avenue
New York, NY 10016
www.hippocrenebooks.com

Library of Congress Cataloging-in-Publication Data
Thompson, Hanne-Ruth.
Bengali (Bangla)-English/English-Bengali (Bangla) dictionary & phrasebook / Hanne-Ruth Thompson.
p. cm.
English and Bengali text.
ISBN-13: 978-0-7818-1252-8 (pbk.)
ISBN-10: 0-7818-1252-6 (pbk.)
1. Bengali language--Dictionaries--English. 2. English language--Dictionaries--Bengali. 3. Bengali language--Conversation and phrase books--English. 4. Bengali language--Textbooks for foreign speakers--English. I. Title. II. Title: Bengali (Bangla)-English/English-Bengali (Bangla) dictionary and phrasebook.
PK1987.T56 2010
491'.4482421--dc22

2010002442

Printed in the United States of America.

CONTENT

INTRODUCTION

Bengali—or Bangla, as it is more appropriately known—is the national language of Bangladesh and the state language of West Bengal, India. There are sizeable Bengali communities in the United States, the United Kingdom, and many other countries all over the world. By numbers of speakers, Bangla is the fifth or sixth most-spoken language in the world. It is related to languages like Hindi and Nepali but has its own script, its own history, its own world-renowned Nobel prize-winning poet, Rabindranath Tagore, and its own particular charm.

There is more tourism (and more English!) in West Bengal than there is in Bangladesh, so this book is perhaps particularly useful for travelers to Bangladesh, a country of great vibrancy and natural beauty and well worth a visit. As this is a dictionary and phrasebook, I have not added a lot of cultural background. It will be helpful to read up on that in other places.

In the hope that this book will inspire readers to move on to further exploration, the Bangla–English dictionary section is given in Bangla alphabetical order. A phonetic transcript is given throughout the book. Further readings are given on page 12. Note that numbers, declined pronoun forms, and kinship terms are not given in the glossary.

ABBREVIATIONS

adj	adjective
adv	adverb
cl	classifier
conj	conjunction
def	definite
emp	emphasiser
expr	expressing
f	female
fam	familiar
hon	honorific
indef	indefinite
instr	instrumental
m	male
musl	Muslim
n	noun
num	number
onom	onomatopoeia
ord	ordinary
pl	plural
pol	polite
pp	postposition
prep	preposition
pr	pronoun
pron	pronounced
PT	phonetic transcript
sg	singular
TL	transliteration
vb	verb

BANGLA ALPHABET

The order of the Bangla alphabet is very systematic. The vowels come first and the consonants are arranged according to position in the mouth and articulation. Bangla reads from left to right and does not distinguish uppercase and lowercase letters.

There are two systems for representing a foreign script in Roman letters. One is a transliteration (TL). This assigns a letter or symbol to each Bangla letter so that the Bangla spelling is accurately reflected. It is a one-by-one representation of Bangla spelling. It does not, however, always tell us how the Bangla words are pronounced.

The second system is a phonetic transcript (PT). This focusses on the sounds of Bangla and aims to represent the pronunciation of Bangla words as closely as possible. Bangla spelling is mostly phonetic, so for the majority of letters there is no conflict between the two systems. However, Bangla has some letters which are pronounced the same, eg. there are two letters pronounced n (ন and ণ), two letters pronounced j (জ and য) and three letters pronounced sh (শ, ষ and স). The phonetic transcript gives us the pronunciation and ignores the graphemic differences. There are also some Bangla letters, particularly the vowels, which have two or even three different pronunciations. A phonetic transcript (PT) shows these differences.

The Bangla alphabetical order of letters follows. For the purpose of this chart, both the transliteration (TL) and the phonetic transcript (PT) are given. B stands for Bangla. The remainder of the book uses a phonetic transcript only.

Vowels

B	TL	PT
অ	ɔ	ɔ, o
আ	a	a, aː
ই	i	i, iː
ঈ	ī	i, iː
উ	u	u, uː
ঊ	ū	u, uː
ঋ	ṙ	ri
এ	e	e, æ
ঐ	oi	oi
ও	o	o
ঔ	ou	ou

Other Symbols

B	TL	PT
ঁ	~	nasal ~
্য	y	(*doubles a consonant, pronounced* a *or* æ *as a vowel*)
ঃ	ḥ	(*not pronounced*)

Consonants

B	TL	PT
ক	k	k
খ	kh	kh
গ	g	g
ঘ	gh	gh
ঙ ṅ	ং ṁ	ng
চ	c	c

B	TL	PT
ছ	ch	ch
জ	j	j
ঝ	jh	jh
ঞ	ñ	ñ
ট	ṭ	ṭ
ঠ	ṭh	ṭh
ড	ḍ	ḍ
ড়	ṛ	ṛ
ঢ	ḍh	ḍh
ঢ়	ṛh	ṛh
ণ	ṇ	n
ত t	ৎ t̲	t
থ	th	th
দ	d	d
ধ	dh	dh
ন	n	n
প	p	p
ফ	ph	ph
ব	b	b
ভ	bh	bh
ম	m	m
য	y	j
য়	ŷ	y
র	r	r
ল	l	l
শ	ś	sh
ষ	ṣ	sh
স	s	sh, s
হ	h	h

Bangla also has a great number of conjuncts which combine two or more consonants in one symbol. Below are some of the more frequent ones. Most of the pronunciations are as expected from the spellings. The unpredictable ones are indicated here.

Conjunct	**Components**	**TL**	**PT**
ক্ত	ক + ত	k + t	kt
ক্র	ক + র	k + r	kr
ক্ষ	ক + ষ	k + ṣ	kkh
গ্ধ	গ + ধ	g + dh	gdh
গ্র	গ + র	g + r	gr
ঙ্ক	ঙ + ক	ṅ + k	nk
ঙ্গ	ঙ + গ	ṅ + g	ngg *as in* fi**ng**er
চ্চ	চ + চ	c + c	*as in* Pu**cc**ini
চ্ছ	চ +ছ	c + ch	*as in* ma**tch**
জ্জ	জ + জ	j + j	jj
জ্ঞ	জ + ঞ	j + ñ	gg
ঞ্চ	ঞ + চ	ñ + c	*as in* po**nch**o
ঞ্জ	ঞ + জ	ñ + j	*as in* ba**nj**o
ণ্ড	ণ + ড	ṇ + ḍ	nḍ *as in* ki**nd**
ত্ত	ত + ত	t + t	tt *as in* do**tt**ore
ত্র	ত + র	t + r	tr
ন্ত	ন + ত	n + t	nt
ন্ত্র	ন + ত + র	n + t + r	ntr
ন্দ	ন + দ	n + d	nd
ন্ন	ন + ন	n + n	nn
প্ত	প + ত	p + t	pt
প্র	প + র	p + r	pr
ম্প	ম + প	m + p	mp

ম্ম	ম + ম	m + m	mm
র্ক	র + ক	r + k	rk
শ্ব	শ + ব	ś + b	sh or ssh
ষ্ট	ষ + ট	ṣ + ṭ	shṭ
স্ত	স + ত	s + t	st
স্ত্র	স + ত + র	s + t + r	str
স্ব	স + ব	s + b	sh or ssh
হ্ন	হ + ন	h + n	nh *as in* pi**nh**ead

Phonetic transcript (PT) and pronunciation

Bangla is a syllabic language which means that consonants cannot stand on their own but are always accompanied by a vowel. Where no vowel is attached to a consonant the inherent vowel অ ɔ or o is often pronounced, as in খবর = kh + b + r, pronounced khɔbor. The inherent vowel is not usually pronounced after the final consonant of a word, eg. নাম is pronounced nam, not namo.

All vowels in Bangla, except the inherent vowel অ ɔ/o have two symbols, (a) a full vowel which stands on its own at the beginning of words and syllables (eg. ঈগল igol *eagle*; উকুন ukun *louse*); and (b) a vowel sign which is attached to consonants. Vowel signs are attached to consonants in varying positions: after, before, underneath, or around the consonants. The resulting consonant-vowel combination forms a syllabic unit. This means that even though the vowel sign can precede the consonant, the consonant is always pronounced first, eg. ি - i + ম - m = মি pronounced mi.

Unlike English vowels, Bangla vowels are pure single sounds, which can be open (or short) as in *pat, pet, pit, pot, put* or closed (or long). For the closed sounds it is difficult to find English equivalents as English sounds tend to shift from one vowel to the other. For instance, the vowel sound in English *go* shifts from e to o to u. Bangla sounds stay in one place. This will need some practice. In order to give a faithful representation of Bangla sounds, some foreign equivalents have been given in the chart below in addition to the description of the sounds.

Vowels

Please read the following section carefully in order to avoid mispronunciations. Note that c in the transcript is always pronounced as in ***chin***, never as in ***ch****aracter*.

The inherent vowel is pronounced either open ɔ as in *on, hot* বলা bɔla or closed o as in *Roma* (Italian pronunciation) ছবি chobi. These pronunciations are given in the transcript. Note that the o pronunciation of the inherent vowel is the same as that of the letter ও o.

All other single vowels, except for ঋ ri can be pronounced long or short. Long pronunciations are particularly common in one-syllable words. Long vowels have a colon added after them in the transcript. Examples are given below.

Vowels

B	TL	PT		B	PT	
অ, –	ɔ	ɔ	open as in ***o**n, h**o**t*	বলা	bɔla	*or*
		o	closed as in Italian *R**o**ma*	ছবি	chobi	
আ, া	a	a	short as in *s**a**mba*	রান্না	ranna	*or*
		a:	long as in *ll**a**ma*	আম	a:m	
ই, ি	i	i	short as in *h**i**t*	জিনিস	jinis	*or*
		i:	long as in *b**ee***	ইদ	i:d	
ঈ, ী	ī	i	short as in *h**i**t*	দীর্ঘ	dirgho	*or*
		i	long as in *b**ee***	নীল	ni:l	
উ, ু	u	u	short as in *p**u**t*	মুক্তি	mukti	*or*
		u:	long as in *r**u**de*	দুধ	du:dh	
ঊ, ূ	ū	u	short as in *p**u**t*	মূল্য	mullo	*or*
		u:	long as in *r**u**de*	দূর	du:r	
ঋ, ৃ	ṙ	ri	this counts as a vowel	তৃপ্ত	tripto	

B	TL	PT		B	PT	
এ, ে	e	e	short as in ***me**t*	কেনা	kena	*or*
		e:	long as in French *ch**e**z*	সে	se	*or*
		æ	open as in *c**a**t*	দেখা	dækha	
ঐ, ৈ	oi	oi	diphthong: closed o followed by i as in Italian ***boi**cotto*	তৈরি	toiri	
ও, ে া	o	o	closed o as in Spanish *c**o**mo*	লোক	lok	
ঔ, ে ৗ	ou	ou	diphthong: closed o followed by u	পৌনে	poune	

Consonants

B	TL	PT		B	PT
ক	k	k	soft k, no aspiration	কলা	kɔla
খ	kh	kh	aspirated k: k + h as in *bac**kh**and*	খেলা	khæla
গ	g	g	soft g, no aspiration	গলা	gɔla
ঘ	gh	gh	aspirated g: g + h as in *do**gh**ouse*	ঘর	ghɔr
ঙ	ṅ	ng	ng as in *si**ng**er* or in *fi**ng**er*	ভাঙা	bhasha
চ	c	c	ch as in ***ch**ip*, little aspiration, also pronounced ts as in *ca**ts***	চাবি	cabi

ছ	ch	ch	ch + h as in *wi**tchh**unt*	ছবি	chobi
জ	j	j	j as in ***j**am*	জল	jɔl
ঝ	jh	jh	aspirated j: j + h as in *he**dgeh**og*	ঝাল	jhal
ঞ	ñ	ñ	nasal n, only used in conjuncts with other letters, eg. ঞ (ñ) + চ (c) = ঞ্চ (ñc)	চঞ্চল	cɔncol
ট	ṭ	ṭ	palatal t, similar to English t as in ***t**op*, but with the tongue slightly further back in the mouth	টাকা	ṭaka
ঠ	ṭh	ṭh	aspirated, palatal t	ঠেলা	ṭhæla
ড	ḍ	ḍ	palatal d, similar to English d as in ***d**ay*, but with the tongue slightly further back in the mouth	ডাল	ḍal
ড়	ṛ	ṛ	a flapped r (*needs practice*)	আড়াই	aṛai
ঢ	ḍh	ḍh	aspirated: palatal d	ঢালা	ḍhala

B	TL	PT		B	PT
ঢ়	ṛh	ṛh	aspirated: flapped r	গাঢ়	gaṛho
ণ	ṇ	n	n as in ***n**ot*	কারণ	karon
ত	t	t	dental t (as in Italian ***t**anto*, the tongue is at the back of the teeth)	তুমি	tumi
ৎ	t̲	t	pronounced as dental t	সৎ	sot
থ	th	th	aspirated: dental t + h	থামা	thama
দ	d	d	soft dental d as in Italian ***d**io*	দল	dɔl
ধ	dh	dh	aspirated: dental d + h	ধান	dhan
ন	n	n	n as in ***n**ot*	না	na
প	p	p	as English p, but without aspiration	পান	pan
ফ	ph	ph	pronounced as pf or f	ফল	phɔl
ব	b	b	as English b in ***b**it*	বাবা	baba
ভ	bh	bh	aspirated b: b+ h as in *da**b** **h**and*	ভুল	bhu:l

ম	m	m	as English m in ***man***	মামা	mama
য	y	j	pronounced as j in ***jam***	যদি	jodi
য়	ŷ	y, w	a semi-vowel (glide) used after vowels, pronounced y as in *ma**y**or* or w as in *a**w**ay*	মেয়ে হাওয়া	meye haowa
র	r	r	rolled r, similar to Italian r	রাগ	ra:g
ল	l	l	as English initial l in ***l**ine,* formed at the front of the mouth	লাল	la:l
শ	ś	sh, s	pronounced as sh in ***sh**ine,* in some conjuncts s as in ***s**un*	শাক	sha:k
ষ	ṣ	sh	pronounced sh as in ***sh**ine*	ষোল	sholo
স	s	sh, s	pronounced sh as in ***sh**ine,* in some conjuncts s as in ***s**un*	সাপ	sha:p
হ	h	h	h as in ***h**ot*	হাত	ha:t

Note: In addition to these, Bangla has some other symbols which are not explained here as they are less important for the pronunciation of words.

FURTHER READING

The following books are useful for learning more Bangla:

Dakshi, Alibha. *Learning Bengali.* Shri K.C. Datta, Kolkata 1995.

Lonely Planet. *Hindi, Urdu, Bengali Phrasebook*: Victoria, Australia 2005.

Nasrin, Mithun and van der Wurff, Wim. *Colloquial Bengali*: Routledge, London 2009.

Radice, William. *Teach Yourself Bengali*: Hodder Headline, London 2007 (3rd ed.).

Seely, Clinton. *Intermediate Bangla*: Lincom Language Course-books, Munich 2002.

Smith, W.L. *Bengali Reference Grammar*: Stockholm Oriental Textbook Series, 1997.

Thompson, Hanne-Ruth. *Essential Everyday Bengali*: Bangla Academy, Dhaka 2006 (2nd ed.).

Thompson, Hanne-Ruth. *Bengali Practical Dictionary*: Hippocrene, New York, 2010.

Thompson, Hanne-Ruth. *Comprehensive Bengali Grammar*: Routledge, London 2010.

GRAMMAR OVERVIEW

WORD ORDER

Basic word order in Bangla is S (Subject) O (Object) V (Verb):

আমি	কাজ	করি।
ami	kaj	kori
I	work	do

I work.

সে	রিনাকে	ভালোবাসে।
she	rimake	bhalobashe
He	Rina + *obj*	loves

He loves Rina.

Due to case endings and verb conjugation, however, word order in Bangla is relatively flexible.

Equational sentences such as *He is my friend* or *Today is Wednesday* have a zero verb in Bangla:

তুমি	আমার বন্ধু।
tumi	amar bondhu
You	my friend

You are my friend.

আজ	বুধবার।
aj	budhbar
today	Wednesday

Today is Wednesday.

Zero verb sentences are negated with the incomplete verb ন:

তুমি আমার বন্ধু নও।
tumi amar bondhu nɔo.
You are not my friend.

আজ বুধবার নয়।
aj budhbar nɔy.
Today is not Wednesday.

Existential/locative structures (*There are problems / We are here*) and possessive structures (*I have a bicycle*) are formed with the incomplete verb আছ্ ach- *be, exist*:

সমস্যা	আছে।
shɔmossha	ache
problems	exist

There are problems.

আমরা	এখানে	আছি।
amra	ekhane	achi
We	here	are

We are here.

আমার	সাইকেল	আছে।
amar	saikel	ache
Of me	bicycle	exists

I have a bicycle.

These sentences are negated with the invariable নেই for all persons:

সমস্যা নেই।
shɔmossha nei.
There are no problems.

তারা এখানে নেই।
tara ekhane nei.
They are not here.

আমার সাইকেল নেই।
amar saikel nei.
I don't have a bicycle.

There are a great number of impersonal structures in Bangla, particularly for expressing feelings and sensations. Impersonal structures do not have agreement between a nominative subject and the verb. The subject in these sentences is often in the genitive.

তার	খারাপ	লাগছে।
tar	kharap	lagche
of him	bad	is attaching

He is feeling ill.

তোমার	কি	শীত	করছে?
tomar	ki	shi:t	korche
of you	what	cold	is making

Are you feeling cold?

তার	ভয়	পেয়ে	গেছে।
tar	bhɔy	peye	gæche
of him	fear	having got	has gone

He got scared.

Nouns

Nouns have four cases: nominative, genitive, objective, locative. Inanimate nouns (things) do not usually take the object case ending. Animate nouns (people) do not usually take the locative. The locative has no plural forms.

Nominative

singular: no ending
plural: -গুলো -gulo, -রা -ra
বইগুলো boigulo *books*
মেয়েরা meyera *girls*

Genitive

singular: র -r, এর -er
বাবার babar *father's*
বাড়ির baṛir *of the home*
বোনের boner *sister's*
plural: -দের der (for people)
গুলোর gulor (for things)
লোকদের lokder *of the people*
গানগুলোর gangulor *of the songs*

Objective

singular: -কে -ke
মানুষকে manushke *to the person*
plural: -দের -der, দেরকে derke
বাচ্চাদের baccader *to the children*
ছেলেদেরকে chelederke *to the boys*

Locative

-এ e, -তে -te -য় -y
গ্রামে grame *in the village*
নদীতে nodite *on the river*
থানায় thanay *at the police station*

Classifiers টা ṭa, টি ṭi, জন jɔn, খানা khana, গুলো gulo, গুলি guli are attached to nouns to form definite and indefinite noun phrases and to distinguish singular and plural. They can, unlike articles in English, occur with possessive adjectives and demonstratives.

আমার	এই	কলমটা
amar	ei	kɔlomṭa
my	this	pen + *cl*

this pen of mine

When a quantifier *(much, many, some, a little)* or a numeral precedes the noun, the classifier is added to it, not to the noun.

অনেকটা পানি
ɔnekṭa pani
much + cl water
a lot of water

পাঁচটা বই
pãcṭa boi
five + cl book
five books

Indefinite noun phrases are formed by adding the singular classifier to the word এক (one):

def: মানুষটি manushṭi *the person*
indef: একটি মানুষ ekṭi manush *a person*

def: কলমটা kɔlomṭa *the pen*
indef: একটা কলম ækṭa kɔlom *a pen*

def: বইখানা boikhana *the book*
indef: একখানা বই ækkhana boi *a book*

For plural indefinites no classifier is used:

def: মানুষগুলো manushgulo *the people*
indef: মানুষ manush *people*

def: কলমগুলি kɔlomguli *the pens*
indef: কলম kɔlom *pens*

Pronouns

Personal pronouns

Bangla pronouns do not distinguish male and female. সে she (ordinary) and তিনি tini (polite) can mean both *he* and *she.* Third person forms distinguish proximity: এ e *this one here,* ও o *that one there,* সে she: *he, she, it* (neutral).

Nominative (subject) *(I, you, he)*

	Singular	**Plural**
1st person	আমি ami	আমরা amra
2nd person familiar	তুমি tumi	তোমরা tomra
2nd person intimate	তুই tui	তোরা tora
2nd person polite	আপনি apni	আপনারা apnara
3rd person ordinary	সে she:	তারা tara
	এ e:	এরা era
	ও o	ওরা ora
3rd person honorific	তিনি tini	তাঁরা tãra
	ইনি ini	এঁরা ẽra
	উনি uni	ওঁরা õra

Genitive (possessive) *(my, our, their)*

	Singular	**Plural**
1st person	আমার amar	আমাদের amader
2nd person familiar	তোমার tomar	তোমাদের tomader
2nd person intimate	তোর tor	তোদের toder
2nd person polite	আপনার apnar	আপনাদের apnader
3rd person ordinary	তার tar	তাদের tader
	এর er	এদের eder
	ওর or	ওদের oder
3rd person honorific	তাঁর tãr	তাঁদের tãder
	এঁর ẽr	এঁদের ẽder
	ওঁর õr	ওঁদের õder

Objective (indirect and direct object)
(*to me, him, them*)

	Singular	**Plural**
1st person	আমাকে amake	আমাদের amader
2nd person familiar	তোমাকে tomake	তোমাদের tomader
2nd person intimate	তোকে toke	তোদের toder
2nd person polite	আপনাকে apnake	আপনাদের apnader
3rd person ordinary	তাকে take	তাদের tader
	একে eke	এদের eder
	ওকে oke	ওদের oder
3rd person honorific	তাঁকে tãke	তাঁদের tãder
	এঁকে ẽke	এঁদের ẽder
	ওঁকে õke	ওঁদের õder

There are some more, alternative forms, particularly for 3rd person plural, but the forms given above are sufficient for learners.

VERBS

Verb conjugation is very regular. Verbs are conjugated according to person and tense. There is no difference between singular and plural verb endings and no gender distinction either in pronouns or in verb forms.

We distinguish three forms for the second person (*you*): familiar (তুমি tumi, তোমরা tomra), intimate (তুই tui, তোরা tora), and polite (আপনি apni, আপনারা apnara); and two forms for third person (*he, she*): ordinary (সে she) and honorific (তিনি tini). Second person polite and third person honorific conjugate the same.

There is a regular vowel shift from high to low stem in simple present verb forms:

আমি লিখি ami likhi *I write*
তুমি লেখ tumi lekho *you write*

আমি দেখি ami dekhi *I see*
তুমি দেখ tumi dækho *you see*

আমি বুঝি ami bujhi *I understand*
তুমি বোঝ tumi bojho *you understand*

আমি বলি ami boli *I say*
তুমি বল tumi bɔlo *you say*

Bangla has eight tenses: simple present, present continuous, present perfect, future tense, simple past, past continuous, past perfect, past habitual.

For specific verb forms the endings for tense and person are added to the stem of the verb.

Verb endings

Present tenses

1st person	i
2nd person familiar	o
3rd person ordinary	e
2nd and 3rd person honorific	en

Past tenses (tense marker l)
Past habit (tense marker t)

1st person	am
2nd person familiar	e
3rd person ordinary	o
2nd and 3rd person honorific	en

Future (tense marker b)

1st person	o
2nd person familiar	e
3rd person ordinary	e
2nd and 3rd person honorific	en

Examples for verb forms in use can be found throughout the phrasebook.

Non-finite verb forms

Every Bangla verb has four non-finite verb forms. They have a variety of uses and occur in connection with finite (conjugated) verb forms. Below are the forms for some common verbs.

(1) verbal noun (low stem):

করা kɔra *doing*
যাওয়া jaowa *going*
খাওয়া khaowa *eating*
থাকা thaka *staying*
বোঝা bojha *understanding*
চেনা cena *recognising*
দেখানো dækhano *showing*

(2) infinitive (high stem):

করতে korte *to do*
যেতে jete *to go*
খেতে khete *to eat*
থাকতে thakte *to stay*
বুঝতে bujhte *to understand*
চিনতে cinte *to recognise*
দেখাতে dækhate *to show*

(3) perfective (or past) participle (high stem):

করে kore *having done*
গিয়ে giye *having gone*
খেয়ে kheye *having eaten*
থেকে theke *having stayed,* also *from*
বুঝে bujhe *having understood*
চিনে cine *having recognised*
দেখিয়ে dekhiye *having shown*

(4) conditional participle (high stem):

করলে korle *if/when you do*

গেলে gele *if/when you go*
খেলে khele *if/when you eat*
থাকলে thakle *if/when you stay*
বুঝলে bujhle *if/when you understand*
চিনলে cinle *if/when you recognise*
দেখালে dækhale *if/when you show*

Non-finite verb forms play an important part in Bangla sentence dynamics, for example:

(1) The verbal noun can be used as the subject in equational sentences.

সব সময় সত্যি কথা বলা কঠিন।
shɔb shɔmɔy shotti kɔtha bɔla kothin.
It is difficult to always tell the truth.

Impersonal passives are constructed with the verbal noun and the verb হওয়া *be, become* or যাওয়া *go*

এই দেশে ধান চাষ করা হয়।
ei deshe dhan cash kɔra hɔy.
Rice is grown in this country.

ইংল্যান্ডে কলা চাষ করা যায় না।
inglænde kɔla cash kɔra jay na.
It is not possible to grow bananas in England.

(2) The infinitive is used with পারা *be able to,* চাওয়া *want*, and verbs expressing purpose.

আমি কালকে আসতে পারব না।
ami kalke ashte parbo na.
I won't be able to come tomorrow.

সে তোমাকে ধন্যবাদ দিতে এসেছে।
she tomake dhɔnnobad dite esheche.
He has come to thank you.

(3) The perfective participle is used in sequences of events and in compound verbs.

সে এই কথা বলে গেছে।
she ei kɔtha bole gæche.
He said this and left.

বইটা শেষ করে তোমার কাছে পাঠাব।
boiṭa shesh kore tomar kache paṭhabo.
I will send you the book when I have finished it.

গাছটা পড়ে গেছে।
gachṭa poṛe gæche.
The tree has fallen down.

লোকটি বসে উঠল।
lokṭi boshe uṭhlo.
The man sat up.

মেয়েটি হেসে ফেলল।
meyeṭi heshe phello.
The girl laughed.

তাকে নিয়ে এস।
take niye esho.
Bring her with you.

(4) The conditional participle can form its own clause.

আমরা তাড়াতাড়ি গেলে
amra taṛataṛi gele
if we go quickly

বৃষ্টি হলে
brishṭi hole
if it rains

তোমার অসুখ ভাল হয়ে গেলে
tomar ɔshukh bhalo hoye gele
when you are well again

ADJECTIVES

Adjectives can be used attributively before the noun:

একটা ভাল কলম
ækṭa bhalo kɔlom
a good pen

এই অদ্ভুত লোকটি
ei odbhut lokṭi
this strange person

আমার লাল শাড়ি
amar la:l shaṛi
my red saree

or predicatively in equational structures:

তাদের বাড়ি খুব সুন্দর।
tader baṛi khub shundor.
Their house is very beautiful.

আমার সাইকেল ভাঙা।
amar saikel bhangga.
My bicycle is broken.

Comparisons are formed with simple adjective forms:

তুমি	আমার চেয়ে	বুদ্ধিমান
tumi	amar ceye	buddhiman
you	than me	intelligent

You are more intelligent than me.

No comparative or superlative adjective forms need to be learned. Comparatives are formed with আরও aro *more* and চেয়ে ceye *more than*; superlatives are formed with সবচেয়ে shɔbceye *than all.*

ভাল bhalo *good*
আরও ভাল aro bhalo *better*
সবচেয়ে ভাল shɔbceye bhalo *best*

সে তোমার চেয়ে লম্বা।
she: tomar ceye lɔmba
He is taller than you.

Equal comparisons are formed with the postposition মত mɔto *like*:

আকাশের মত বড়
akasher mɔto bɔṛo
as big as the sky

তার মত সুন্দর
tar mɔto sundor
as beautiful as she

ADVERBS

Adverbs can be formed from adjectives by adding করে kore *having done* or ভাবে bhabe *in the way*:

নরম nɔrom *soft* — নরমভাবে nɔrombhabe *softly*
ভাল bhalo *good* — ভাল করে bhalo kore *well*

Adding এ *e* to some nouns and adjectives produces adverbs:

সহজ shɔhoj *easy* — সহজে shɔhoje *easily*
আসল ashol *actual* — আসলে ashole *actually*
গোপন gopon *hidden* — গোপনে gopone *secretly*

Some adverbs are formed from nouns and adjectives by adding -ɔto:

বিশেষত bisheshɔto *especially*
সাধারণত shadharonɔto *usually*
প্রধানত prodhanɔto *mainly*
সম্ভবত sɔmbhobɔto *possibly*

but there are also a great number of underived adverbs, such as:

দারুণ darun *very*
ধীরে dhire *slowly*
আবার abar *again*
বেশ besh *quite*
প্রায় pray *almost*
মাত্র matro *only*
আস্তে aste *slowly*
খুব khub *very*
হঠাৎ hɔṭhat *suddenly*
ভীষণ bhishon *extremely*
শুধু shudhu *only*
কেবল kebol *only*

INTERROGATIVES (QUESTION WORDS)

Interrogatives do not make up a word class on their own. They are pronouns, adjectives, and adverbs. The main question words are:

কে ke: *who*
কি ki: *what*
কেন kæno *why*
কেমন kæmon *how*
কোথায় kothay *where*
কবে kɔbe *when*
কখন kɔkhon *when*
কোন kon *which*
কত kɔto *how much*
কয়টা kɔyṭa *how many*

Postpositions

Postpositions are equivalent to prepositions *(in, on, with, over, for, etc.)* and appear after the noun they position. Most Bangla spatial postpositions are locative noun forms and require a preceding genitive:

টেবিলের	উপরে
ṭebiler	upore
of the table	on top
on the table	

Some postpositions are derived from verbs – the preceding noun is in the nominative:

ছুরি	দিয়ে
churi	diye
knife	having given = with
with a knife	

রান্না-ঘর	থেকে
ranna-ghɔr	theke
kitchen	having stayed = from
from the kitchen	

There are also some non-derived postpositions whose case uses need to be learned:

মত mɔto *as, like* with preceding genitive:
বিজলির মত bijolir mɔto *like lightning*

পর্যন্ত porjonto *until* with preceding nominative:
সোমবার পর্যন্ত shombar porjonto *until Monday*

জন্য jɔnno, জন্যে jɔnne *for* with preceding genitive:
তোমার জন্যে tomar jɔnne *for you*

Conjunctions (Joining words)

Bangla has three ways of joining sentences:

(1) with coordinating conjunctions to connect two main clauses:

আর ar *and*
এবং ebɔng *and*
কিন্তু kintu *but*
বা ba *or*
কারণ karon *because*
সুতরাং shutorang *hence, therefore*
কাজেই kajei *so, therefore*
তাই tai *so, therefore*
তবে tɔbe *but*
তারপর tarpɔr *then, afterwards*

খালি হাঁ করে আর চিঁ চিঁ করে।
khali hã kore ar cĩ cĩ kore
They just open their mouths and go chee chee.

ওরা এসেছিলো কিন্তু আমাদের সঙ্গে দেখা করেনি।
ora eshechilo kintu amader shɔngge dækha kɔreni.
They came but didn't meet with us.

(2) with single subordinating conjunctions (there are very few of those) to join a subordinate clause to a main clause:

যে je *that*
যেন jæno *so that*
যাতে jate *so that*
পাছে pache *so that not*
বলে bole *that*

মনে হত যেন কোনও কিছু আমাকে দুঃখ দিতে পারবে না।
mone holo jæno kono kichu amake dukho dite parbe na.

It seemed to me that nothing could possibly make me sad.

তারা জানেও না যে কেন তারা পৃথিবীতে এসেছে।
tara janeo na je kæno tara prithibite esheche.
They don't even know why they have come into the world.

টাকা দিয়েছি তাকে, তার প্রয়োজন ছিল বলেই।
ṭaka diyechi take, tar proyojon chilo bolei
I gave him the money because he needed it.

(3) with correlative conjunctions or pronouns

Correlative structures usually have a preceding subordinate clause, with a relative conjunction/pronoun, followed by the correlative pronoun/conjunction introducing the main clause. In the following sentences the relative and correlative words are underlined to show the structures.

তারা <u>যখন</u> আসবে <u>তখন</u> আমি পোলাও খাওয়াব।
tara <u>jɔkhon</u> ashbe <u>tɔkhon</u> ami polao khaowabo.
When they come I will give them Pilao to eat.

আমি সে দিন <u>যা</u> দেখলাম <u>তা</u> চিরদিন মনে থাকবে।
ami she di:n <u>ja</u> dekhlam <u>ta</u> cirodi:n mone thakbe.
I will remember forever what I saw that day.

তুমি <u>যদি</u> আরও থাকতে না চাও <u>তাহলে</u> চলে যেতে পারবে।
tumi <u>jodi</u> aro thakte na cao <u>tahole</u> cole jete parbe.
If you don't want to stay any longer you can leave.

PARTICLES

Particles are words which are not syntactically necessary but have a decisive influence on the perspective or attitude of a sentence or statement. They are not usually translatable as individual words but gain their meaning in context. Common particles are:

তো to তোমাকেই তো সবই বলি।
tomake to sɔbi boli.
But I tell you everything.

ই i আমি কিছুই করিনি।
ami kichui korini.
I didn't do anything at all.

ও o তিনি তাও জানতেন না।
tini tao janten na.
He didn't even know that.

তা ta তা কি বলছ?
ta ki bolcho?
What exactly are you saying?

বা ba তুমিই বা যাবে কেন?
tumii ba jabe kæno?
Why on earth would you go?

যে je তার সঙ্গে আজ দেখা হয়নি যে।
tar shɔngge a:j dækha hɔyni je.
I didn't see him today — that's why.

INTERJECTIONS

Interjections are similar to particles in that they have no syntactic role but they express the speaker's feelings and their use is restricted to direct speech. Below are a few with the emotions they express:

ছিঃ *disgust*
ছিঃ ! তুমি আমাকে এই নামে আর ডাকবে না।
chi! tumi amake ei name ar ḍakbe na.
Oh please! Don't call me by that name again.

হায়রে *despair or exasperation*

হায়রে, আর কতক্ষণ?

hayre, ar kɔtokkhɔn?

Oh for heaven's sake, how much longer?

মাগো *pity*

মাগো, ছেলেটিকে দেখেছো?

mago, cheleṭike dekhecho?

Oh dear, did you see the boy?

দূর *impatience*

দূর হও, আবার এই কথা!

du:r hɔo, abar ei kɔtha!

Really, not that again!

ONOMATOPOEAIA

One characteristic feature of Bangla is its rich stock of onomatopoeia, words which represent sounds, emotions, visual and other sensory impressions. These words are often doubled. Onomatopoeia add color and spice to the language and are an essential ingredient of Bengali literature.

আমি থরথর করে কাঁপছিলাম।

ami thɔrthɔr kore kãpchilam.

I was shivering violently.

সে ফিসফিস করে বলল।

she phishphish kore bollo.

He spoke in a whisper.

বাচ্চাটি ভয়ে হাউমাউ করে কেঁদে উঠল।

baccaṭi bhɔye haumau kore kẽde uṭhlo.

The child was so scared that he started wailing.

সব ব্যাপারে এত খুঁতখুঁত হলে চলে না।

shɔb bæpare eto khũtkhũt hole cɔle na.

It won't do to be so petty about everything.

পুকুরের জল টলমল।
pukurer jɔl ṭɔlmɔl.
The water of the lake was churning.

সারা শহর থমথম হয়ে আছে।
shara shɔhor thɔmthɔm hoye ache.
The whole town was eerily silent.

BANGLA – ENGLISH DICTIONARY

The Bangla–English entries are given in Bangla alphabetical order, which is as follows:

অ ɔ/o, আ a, ই i/i: ঈ i/i: উ u/u: ঊ u/u: ঋ ri,
এ e/æ, ঐ oi, ও o, ঔ ou

ং ng, ঃ ḥ, ঁ ~ (nasal)

ক k, খ kh, গ g, ঘ gh, ঙ ng,
চ c, ছ ch, জ j, ঝ jh, ঞ ñ,
ট ṭ, ঠ ṭh, ড ḍ, ড় ṛ, ঢ ḍh, ঢ় ṛh, ণ n,
ত/ৎ t, থ th, দ d, ধ dh, ন n,
প p, ফ ph, ব b, ভ bh, ম m,
য j, য় y, র r, ল l, শ sh, s ষ sh, স sh, s, হ h

অ ɔ/o

অংশ ɔngsho *n* part, share
অংশ নেওয়া ɔngsho neowa *vb* take part
অকারণে ɔkarone *adv* unnecessarily
অঙ্ক ɔnko *n* sum, digit, number
অচেনা ɔcena *adj* unknown, strange
অজানা ɔjana *adj* unknown, strange
অঞ্চল ɔncol *n* region
অত ɔto *adv* so, so much
অতএব ɔtoeb *adv* hence, so, therefore
অতিথি otithi *n* guest
অতিরিক্ত otirikto *adj* surplus, extra, too much
অতীত otit *pp* past, beyond
অত্যাচার ottacar *n* oppression, tyranny

অথচ ɔthoco *conj* yet, still
অথবা ɔthoba *conj* or
অদূর ɔdur *adj* not far, near, close
অদ্ভুত ɔdbhut *adj* strange
অধিকাংশ odhikangsho *adj* most
অধিকার odhikar *n* right, claim
অনিশ্চিত ɔnishcito *adj* uncertain, indefinite
অনুপস্থিত ɔnuposthit *adj* absent, not present
অনুবাদ onubad *n* translation
অনুবাদ করা onubad kɔra *vb* translate
অনুভব onubhɔb *n* perception, feeling
অনুভূতি onubhuti *n* feeling, intuition
অনুমতি onumoti *n* permission, leave
অনুমোদন onumodon *n* consent, approval
অনুষ্ঠান onuṣṭhan *n* ceremony, celebration
অনেক ɔnek *adj* much, many
অনেকক্ষণ ɔnekkhon *adv* a long time
অন্তত ɔntoto *adv* at least
অন্তর ɔntor *n* heart, depth, interior
অন্ধ ɔndho *adj* blind
অন্ধকার ɔndhokar *n* darkness
অন্য ɔnno *adj* other, different
অন্যান্য ɔnnanyo *n, adj* several others
অন্যায় ɔnnay *n* wrong-doing, injustice
অপছন্দ ɔpɔchondo *n* dislike, aversion
অপমান ɔpoman *n* insult, disgrace
অপরাজিত ɔpɔrajito *adj* victorious
অপরাধ ɔporadh *n* fault, crime
অপরিচিত ɔporicito *adj* unknown
অপেক্ষা ɔpekkha *n* wait, delay
অপেক্ষা করা ɔpekkha kɔra *vb* wait
অপ্রয়োজনীয় ɔproyojoniyo *adj* unnecessary
অপ্রস্তুত ɔprostut *adj* unprepared
অবকাশ ɔbokash *n* leisure, respite
অবশেষে ɔbosheshe *adv* finally, at last
অবশ্য ɔbossho *adv* of course

অবসর ɔboshɔr *n* leisure, retirement
অবস্থা ɔbostha *n* situation
অবহেলা ɔbohæla *n* neglect
অবাক ɔbak *adj* amazed, stunned, speechless
অবাস্তব ɔbastob *adj* unreal
অবিবাহিত ɔbibahito *adj* unmarried
অবিশ্বাসী ɔbisshashi *adj* untrustworthy, unfaithful
অবেলা ɔbela *adv* untimely
অভদ্র ɔbhɔdro *adj* impolite, rude, discourteous
অভাব ɔbhab *n* lack, want
অভিজ্ঞতা obhiggota *n* experience
অভিধান obhidhan *n* dictionary
অভিযোগ obhijog *n* complaint, accusation
অভিশাপ obhishap *n* curse
অভ্যাস ɔbbhash *n* habit, custom
অমনি omni *adv* just like that
অমুক omuk *n* someone
অর্থ ɔrtho *n* meaning, significance, wealth
অর্থনীতি ɔrthoniti *n* economics
অর্থাৎ ɔrthat *conj* that is, namely
অর্ধেক ɔrdhek *adj* half
অলস ɔlosh *adj* lazy, idle, indolent
অল্প ɔlpo *adj* a little
অল্প-কিছু ɔlpo kichu *n* a small amount
অল্প বয়সী ɔlpo bɔyoshi *n* young
অশান্তি ɔshanti *n* lack of peace, unrest
অশিক্ষিত ɔshikkhito *adj* illiterate, uneducated
অসৎ ɔshɔt *adj* dishonest
অসন্তুষ্ট ɔshɔntushṭo *adj* displeased, dissatisfied
অসম্পূর্ণ ɔshɔmpurno *adj* incomplete, unfinished
অসম্ভব ɔshɔmbhɔb *adj* impossible
অসহায় ɔshɔhay *adj* defenseless, helpless
অসহ্য ɔshojjo *adj* unbearable
অসাধারণ ɔsadharon *adj* unusual
অসুখ ɔshukh *n* illness
অসুবিধা ɔshubidha *n* inconvenience

অসুস্থ ɔshustho *adj* ill, unwell
অস্ত্র ɔstro *n* instrument, tool
অস্থির ɔsthir *adj* restless, uneasy
অস্বাভাবিক ɔshabhabik *adj* unusual, rare
অস্বীকার ɔsshikar *n* denial, non-acceptance
অহঙ্কার ɔhongkar *n* pride, vanity, arrogance

আ a

আইন ain *n* law, rule
আওয়াজ aowaj *n* sound, voice
আংটি angṭi *n* ring
আঁকা ãka *vb* draw
আঁকাবাঁকা ãkabãka *n* zigzag
আঁচ ã:c *n* guess, conjecture
আকর্ষণ akorshon *n* attraction, pull
আকাঙ্ক্ষা akangkkha *n* ambition, wish
আকার akar *n* shape, form
আকাশ akash *n* sky
আক্রমণ akromon *n* attack
আখ a:kh *n* sugarcane
আগমন agomon *n* arrival
আগামী agami *adj* next, coming
আগুন agun *n* fire
আগে age *adv, pp* before, earlier, in front of
আগ্রহ agroho *n* interest
আঘাত aghat *n* blow, stroke, hit
আঙুর anggur *n* grape
আঙুল anggul *n* finger
আচরণ acoron *n* behavior
আচার acar *n* pickle, chutney
আচ্ছা accha *int* fine, well, OK
আছ- ach- *vb* be, be present, exist
আজ a:j, আজকে ajke *n, adv* today, this day
আজকাল ajkal *adv* nowadays
আজেবাজে ajebaje *adj* nonsense, worthless

আঞ্চলিক ancolik *adj* local, regional
আটকানো aṭkano *vb* confine, obstruct
আটা aṭa *n* coarse flour
আঠা aṭha *n* glue
আঠার aṭharo *n* eighteen
আড়াই aṛai *n* two and a half
আত্মসম্মান attoshɔmman *n* self-respect
আত্মহত্যা attohɔtta *n* suicide
আত্মা atta *n* soul
আত্মীয় -স্বজন attiyo-shɔjon *n* relatives, kin
আদতে adote *adv* in reality, really
আদর ador *n* love, affection, caress
আদর্শ adorsho *n* ideal
আদা ada *n* ginger
আদালত adalɔt *n* court of law
আদেশ adesh *n* order, command
আধ a:dh, আধা adha *n, adj* half
আধুনিক adhunik *adj* modern, current
আনন্দ anondo *n* joy
আনা ana *vb* bring
আনারস anarɔsh *n* pineapple
আন্তরিক antorik *adj* heartfelt, sincere
আপত্তি apotti *n* objection
আপন apon *adj* one's own
আপা apa *n* sister (*older*)
আপাতত apatɔto *adv* at present, for now
আবহাওয়া abhaowa *n* weather
আবার abar *adv* again
আবিস্কার abishkar *n* invention, discovery
আবেগ abeg *n* emotion, passion
আব্বা abba *n* father
আম a:m *n* mango
আম্মা amma *n* mother
আমরা amra *pr* we
আমাশা amasha *n* dysentry
আমি ami *pr* I

আমোদ-প্রমোদ amod-promod *n* recreation, entertainment
আয় ay *n* earnings, income
আয়না ayna *n* mirror
আয়া aya *n* nurse-maid
আর ar *conj* and, also, else, more
আরও aro *conj* more
আরম্ভ করা arombho kɔra *vb* begin
আরাম aram *n* comfort, ease
আলনা alna *n* rack, stand for clothes
আলমারি almari *n* cupboard
আলাদা alada *adj* separate
আলাপ alap *n* conversation
আলাপ করা alap kɔra *vb* talk
আলু alu *n* potato
আলো alo *n* light, beam, ray
আলোচনা alocona *n* discussion, deliberation
আশা asha *n* hope, expectation
আশি ashi *n* eighty
আশীর্বাদ ashirbad *n* blessing, benediction
আশ্চর্য ashcorjo *n* wonder, surprise, marvel
আশ্রয় asrɔy *n* shelter, refuge
আসল ashol *adj* real, genuine, true
আসলে ashole *adv* actually, in fact
আসা asha *vb* come, arrive, reach
আস্তে aste *adv* slowly, softly, carefully
আস্থা astha *n* trust, faith, reliance

ই i/i:

ই i *emp expr emphasis*
ইউরোপ iurop *n* Europe
ইংরেজি ingreji *adj* English (*language*)
ইঙ্গিত inggit *n* sign, hint
ইচ্ছা iccha *n* wish
ইচ্ছা করা iccha kɔra *vb* want, desire
ইট i:ṭ *n* brick

ইতস্তত করা itostoto kɔra *vb* hesitate, procrastinate
ইতি iti *n* end, termination
ইতিমধ্যে itimoddhe *adv* in the meantime
ইতিহাস itihash *n* history
ইত্যাদি ittadi *adv* and so on
ইন্দুর indur *n* rat, mouse
ইস্কুল iskul *n* school
ইস্ত্রি istri *n* iron (clothes-press)

ঈ i/i:

ঈদ i:d *n* Eid
ঈশ্বর isshor *n* God

উ u/u:

উকিল ukil *n* lawyer
উকুন ukun *n* louse
উচিত ucit *adj* proper, right
উচ্চারণ uccaron *n* pronunciation
উট u:ṭ *n* camel
উঠা uṭha (*also* ওঠা oṭha) *vb* rise, get up
উঠান uṭhan *n* courtyard
উড়া uṛa (*also* ওড়া oṛa) *vb* fly
উত্তর uttor *n* answer, reply
উত্তর uttor *n* north
উৎসব utshob *n* ceremony
উদাহরণ udahoron *n* example
উদ্দেশ্য uddessho *n* purpose, aim
উনি uni *pr* he, she (*honorific*)
উন্নত unnoto *adj* prospering, improved
উন্নতি unnoti *n* improvement
উপকার upokar *n* favor, benefit
উপদেশ upodesh *n* advice, counsel
উপর upor *n* top, on top of, on
উপরে upore *pp* on, above

উপস্থিত uposthit *adj* present, arrived
উপহার upohar *n* present, gift
উপায় upay *n* way, method
উলটা ulṭa *adj* upside down
উলটানো ulṭano *vb* turn upside down

ঋ ri

ঋণ ri:n *n* loan, debt
ঋতু ritu *n* season

এ e/æ

এই ei *pr* this
এই তো eito *adv* just this
এই বার ei bar *adv* this time
এইমাত্র eimatro *adv* just now
এক æk *n* one
একঘেয়ে ækgheye *adj* monotonous
একটু ekṭu *adj* a little
একদম ækdom *adv* altogether
একবার ækbar *adv* once
একমাত্র ekmatro *adj* only
একসঙ্গে ekshɔngge *adv* together
একরকম ækrɔkom *adj* similar, same
একতা ækota *n* unity
একলা ækla *adv* alone
একা æka *adj* alone, unaccompanied
একই eki *adj* same
একেবারে ækebare *adv* completely
এক্ষণি ekkhoni *adv* right now
এখন ækhon *adv* now
এখানে ekhane *adv* here
এত æto *adj* so, so much
এতক্ষণ ætokkhon *adv* for so long (*within a day*)
এতদিন ætodin *adv* for so long

এতদূর ætodu:r *adv* so far
এদিক edik *adv* this way
এবং ebɔng *conj* and
এমন æmon *adj* such, so, like this
এমনি emni *adv* just like that, spontaneously
এলাকা elaka *n* area
এলোমেলো elomelo *adj* disorderly

ও o

ও o *pr* he, she; *conj* also
ওই oi *pr* that over there
ওখানকার okhankar *adv* of that place, of that region
ওখানে okhane *adv* there
ওঠা oṭha *vb* rise
ওড়া oṛa *vb* fly
ওরা ora *pr* they
ওষুধ oshudh *n* medicine
ওষুধের দোকান osudher dokan *n* pharmacy

ক k

কই koi *adv* where
কখন kɔkhon *conj* when
কখনও kɔkhono *adv* ever
কচ্ছপ kɔcchop *n* turtle
কঠিন koṭhin *adj* difficult, hard, firm
কড়া kɔṛa *adj* harsh, severe
কড়াই kɔṛai *n* large cooking utensil, pan
কত kɔto *adj* how much, how many
কতক্ষণ kɔtokkhon *adv* for how long
কতদিন kɔtodin *adv* for how long
কথা kɔtha *n* word, fact, statement
কথা দেওয়া kɔtha deowa *vb* promise
কথা বলা kɔtha bɔla *vb* speak
কথা রাখা kɔtha rakha *vb* keep promise

কথাবার্তা kɔthabarta *n* conversation
কথামত kɔthamɔto *adj* as promised
কথামাত্র kɔthamatro *adj* mere words, empty talk
কপি kopi *n* cabbage
কপি kopi *n* copy
কফি kophi *n* coffee
কবি kobi *n* poet
কবিতা kobita *n* poetry
কবে kɔbe *conj* when
কম kɔm *adj* deficient, short
কম পড়া kɔm pɔṛa *vb* fall short
কমপক্ষে kɔmpɔkkhe *adv* at least
কমবেশি kɔmbeshi *adv* more or less
কমলা kɔmla *n, adj* orange
কমা kɔma *vb* decrease
কমানো kɔmano *vb* reduce
কম্বল kɔmbol *n* blanket
কয় kɔy *adj* how many
কয়েক kɔyek *adj* a few
করা kɔra *vb* do, make
করে kore *conj* due to
কল kɔl *n* machine, engine
কলম kɔlom *n* pen
কলসি kolshi *n* pitcher of water
কলা kɔla *n* banana
কলেজ kɔlej *n* college
কল্পনা kɔlpona *n* imagination
কল্পনা করা kɔlpona kɔra *n* imagine, fancy
কষ্ট kɔshṭo *n* trouble, grief, sorrow
কাঁচা kãca *adj* unripe, green, immature, raw
কাঁচি kãci *n* scissors
কাঁটা kãṭa *n* thorn
কাঁঠাল kãṭhal *n* jackfruit
কাঁদা kãda *vb* weep, cry
কাঁধ kãdh *n* shoulder
কাঁপা kãpa *vb* tremble, shiver

কাক ka:k *n* crow
কাগজ kagoj *n* paper
কাচ ka:c *n* glass
কাছ kach *n* proximity
কাছে kache *adv, pp* next to, close to
কাজ ka:j *n* work
কাজের লোক kajer lok *n* servant, employee
কাজেই kajei *conj* so, therefore
কাটা kaṭa *vb* cut; pass
কাটা চামচ kaṭa camoc *n* fork
কাটানো kaṭano *vb* cause to be cut; spend
কাঠ ka:ṭh *n* wood, timber
কাদা kada *n* mud
কান ka:n *n* ear
কানা kana *adj* blind
কাপ kap *n* cup
কাপড় kapoṛ *n* cloth
কাপড়-চোপড় kapoṛcopor *n* clothes
কামড় দেওয়া kamoṛ deowa *vb* bite
কায়দা kayda *n* system, method
কারণ karon *n* reason, cause
কার্ড karḍ *n* card
কাল ka:l *n* time, period
কাল ka:l *adv* tomorrow, yesterday
কাল, কালো kalo *adj* black
কালকে kalke *adv* tomorrow, yesterday
কালজাম kalojam *n* dark cherry
কালা kala *adj* deaf
কালি kali *n* ink
কাহিনী kahini *n* story, anecdote
কাহিল kahil *adj* exhausted, tired
কি ki: *pr* what
কিংবা kingba *conj* or, alternatively
কিছু kichu *n, adj* something, some
কিনা kina *adv* whether or not
কিনারা kinara *n* border

কিন্তু kintu *conj* but
কুকুর kukur *n* dog
কুমড়া kumṛa *n* pumpkin
কুমির kumir *n* crocodile
কুয়াশা kuwasha *n* fog, mist
কুলি kuli *n* porter
কৃষক krishok *n* farmer
কৃষি krishi *n* agriculture
কে ke *pr* who
কেউ keu *pr* someone
কেক kek *n* cake
কেচি keci *n* scissors
কেন kæno *adv* why
কেনা kena *vb* buy
কেন্দ্র kendro *n* center
কেবল kebol *adv* only
কেমন kæmon *adv* how
কেরাসিন kerashin *n* kerosene
কোটি koṭi *n* crore, ten million
কোন kon *adv* which
কোনও kono *adj* any
কোমর komor *n* waist
কোমল komol *adj* soft, gentle
কৌশল koushol *n* skill, dexterity
ক্যামেরা kæmera *n* camera
ক্রিয়া kriya *n* action, work
ক্লান্ত klanto *adj* tired
ক্লাস klash *n* class
ক্ষণ khɔn *n* moment, instant
ক্ষতি khoti *n* harm, damage
ক্ষমতা khɔmota *n* power, strength
ক্ষমা khɔma *n* forgiveness

খ kh

খই khoi *n* puffed rice
খড় khɔṛ *n* hay, straw
খবর khɔbor *n* news
খবরের কাগজ khɔborer kagoj *n* newspaper
খরচ khɔroc *n* expense, spending
খাওয়া khaowa *vb* eat
খাওয়ানো khaowano *vb* feed
খাঁচা khãca *n* cage
খাঁটি khãṭi *adj* pure, unadulterated
খাটো khaṭo *adj* short
খাটনি khaṭni *n* hard work, labor
খাতা khata *n* notebook
খাবার khabar *n* food
খাম kha:m *n* envelope
খারাপ kharap *adj* bad, evil
খালি khali *adj, adv* empty, only
খিদা khida, খিদে khide *n* hunger
খুঁটিনাটি khũṭinaṭi *n* trifle, unimportant matter
খুচরা khucra *n* small change (*money*)
খুব khu:b *adv* very
খুশি khushi *adj* happy
খেয়াল kheyal *n* attention, thought, fancy
খেলা khæla *vb* play; *n* game, sport
খোঁজ khõj *n* search, inquiry
খোঁজা khõja *vb* search, investigate
খোলা khola *vb, adj* open
খ্রিস্টান khrishṭan *n, adj* Christian

গ g

গঙ্গা gɔngga *n* Ganges
গঠন gɔṭhon *n* construction, formation
গড় gɔṛ *n* average

গণ gɔn *n* common people, population
গণতন্ত্র gɔnotɔntro *n* democracy
গণিত gonito *adj* reckoned, counted
গণ্ডগোল gɔnḍogol *n* uproar, tumult, riot, disorder
গত gɔto *adj* departed; last
গতকাল gɔtokal *n* yesterday
গতপর্শু gɔtoporshu *n* day before yesterday
গন্ধ gɔndho *n* smell, scent, odor
গভীর gobhir *adj* deep, extending far down
গম gɔm *n* wheat
গম্ভীর gombhir *adj* serious, grave, solemn
গয়না gɔyna *n* jewelry
গরম gɔrom *n, adj* heat, hot
গরিব gorib *adj* poor
গরু goru *n* cow
গর্ত gɔrto *n* hole, cavity, ditch
গর্বিত gorbito *adj* proud, conceited, vain
গলা gɔla *vb* melt, soften; rot
গলা gɔla *n* throat, neck; voice
গলি goli *n* lane, alley
গল্প gɔlpo *n* story, tale, fable
গল্পগুজব gɔlpogujob *n* gossip, chit-chat
গা ga: *n* body
গায়ে দেওয়া gaye deowa *vb* wear, put on
গাওয়া gaowa *vb* sing
গাছ ga:ch *n* tree, plant
গাজর gajor *n* carrot
গাড়ি gaṛi *n* car, vehicle
গাধা gadha *n* donkey, ass
গান ga:n *n* song
গামছা gamcha *n* thin towel, napkin
গায়ক gayok *n* singer
গাল ga:l *n* cheek
গির্জা girja *n* church
গিলা gila (*also* গেলা gela) *vb* swallow
গু gu: *n* feces, stool, dung

গুছানো guchano *vb* tidy up, arrange
গুজব gujɔb *n* rumor, hearsay
গুড় guṛ *n* juice of sugarcane; molasses
গুণ gu:n *n* quality, virtue
গুপ্ত gupto *adj* secret, hidden, unrevealed
গুপ্তচর guptocɔr *n* spy, detective
গুরু guru *n* teacher, guide, mentor
গুরুত্ব gurutto *n* importance, seriousness
গুরুত্বপূর্ণ guruttopurno *adj* important, serious, weighty
গুলি guli *n* marble; bullet
গুহা guha *n* cave, mountain-cave
গেঞ্জি genji *n* vest; T-Shirt
গেট geṭ *n* gate
গেলাস gelash *n* glass, tumbler
গোঁফ gõph *n* moustache
গোনা gona *vb* count
গোপন gopon *adj* secret, hidden, private; *n* secret
গোল gol *adj* round
গোলমাল golmal *n* riot, tumult, uproar, disturbance
গোলাপ golap *n* rose
গোলাপি golapi *adj* rose-colored, pink
গোসল goshol *n* bath; bathing
গোসলখানা gosholkhana *n* bathroom
গৌরব gourob *n* glory, honor, dignity
গ্যাস gæsh *n* gas
গ্রহণ করা grohon kɔra *vb* accept
গ্রাম gra:m *n* village
গ্রাস gra:sh *n* mouthful, morsel; grip

ঘ gh

ঘটনা ghɔṭona *n* event, occurrence
ঘটা ghɔṭa *vb* occur, happen
ঘড়ি ghoṛi *n* clock, watch
ঘণ্টা ghɔnṭa *n* hour
ঘনিষ্ঠ ghonishṭho *adj* close, intimate

ঘর ghɔr *n* house, building
ঘা gha: *n* wound, stroke, blow
ঘাট gha:ṭ *n* landing stage, quay, wharf, ghat
ঘাড় ghaṛ *n* neck, nape of the neck
ঘাম gha:m *n* sweat
ঘাস gha:s *n* grass
ঘি ghi: *n* ghee, clarified butter
ঘুম ghu:m *n* sleep
ঘুমানো ghumano *vb* sleep
ঘুষ ghu:sh *n* bribe
ঘূর্ণিঝড় ghurnijhɔṛ *n* cyclone, tornado
ঘৃণা ghrina *n* hate, aversion, disgust, revulsion
ঘৃণা করা ghrina kɔra *vb* hate, detest, despise
ঘোড়া ghoṛa *n* horse
ঘোড়ার গাড়ি ghoṛar gaṛi *n* tom-tom; horse-drawn carriage
ঘোরা ghora *vb* turn, move, wander

চ c

চমৎকার cɔmotkar *adj* excellent, good
চরম cɔrom *adj* highest, ultimate
চরিত্র coritro *n* character
চর্চা cɔrca *n* practice, study, application
চলতি colti *adj* current, present, going
চলা cɔla *vb* go, move, run
চলিত colit *adj* colloquial, current
চশমা cɔshma *n* glasses, spectacles
চা ca: *n* tea
চাইতে caite *conj* than
চাউল caul, চাল ca:l *n* uncooked rice
চাওয়া caowa *vb* want, desire, look at
চাঁদ ca:d *n* moon
চাকর cakor *n* servant
চাকরি cakri *n* job, employment
চাকা caka *n* wheel
চাদর cador *n* bedsheet; wrap

চান ca:n *n* bath
চাপ ca:p *n* pressure, weight, burden
চাপা capa *vb* press; suppress
চাপাটি capaṭi *n* flat bread
চাবি cabi *n* key
চামচ camoc *n* spoon
চামড়া camṛa *n* skin, leather
চারা cara *n* seedling, young plant
চালাক calak *adj* clever, cunning
চালানো calano *vb* drive, conduct, lead
চাষ ca:sh *n* agriculture, cultivation
চাষী cashi *n* farmer, plowman
চিংড়ি cingṛi *n* shrimp, prawn
চিকন cikon *adj* fine, thin, delicate
চিকিৎসা cikitsha *n* treatment
চিঠি ciṭhi *n* letter
চিড়িয়াখানা ciṛiyakhana *n* zoo
চিৎকার citkar *n* scream
চিনি cini *n* sugar
চিন্তা cinta *n* thought; worry
চিন্তিত cintito *adj* anxious, worried
চিরুনি ciruni *n* comb
চিহ্ন cinho *n* sign, mark, trace
চুক্তি cukti *n* agreement, contract
চুপ cu:p, চুপচাপ cupcap *adj* silent, mute
চুমু cumu *n* kiss
চুরি curi *n* theft, stealing
চুল cu:l *n* hair
চুলকানো culkano *vb* scratch, itch
চুলা cula *n* oven, cooker
চেক cek *n* check
চেতনা cetona *n* consciousness, sensibility
চেনা cena *vb* know, recognise
চেয়ার ceyar *n* chair
চেয়ে ceye *conj* than
চেষ্টা ceshṭa *n* attempt, effort

চেহারা cehara *n* complexion, appearance, features
চোখ cokh *n* eye
চোর cor *n* thief, robber
চোষা cosha *vb* suck
চৌকিদার coukidar *n* guard, watchman

ছ ch

ছবি chobi *n* picture, painting
ছাই chai *n* ash
ছাঁকা chãka *vb* sieve, strain
ছাগল chagol *n* goat
ছাড়া chaṛa *vb* leave, depart, let go; *pp* except, without
ছাতা chata *n* umbrella; mushroom
ছাতি chati *n* umbrella
ছাত্র chatro *n* student, pupil
ছাদ cha:d *n* roof, ceiling
ছাপা chapa *vb* print, publish
ছায়া chaya *n* shade, shadow
ছুটি chuṭi *n* holiday, leisure
ছুরি churi *n* knife
ছেঁড়া chẽṛa *vb* tear, rip
ছেলে chele *n* boy, son
ছেলেবেলা chelebela *n* childhood
ছোট choṭo *adj* small, young
ছোলা chola *vb* strip, peel

জ j

জংলি jongli *adj* wild
জগ jɔg *n* jug
জগৎ jɔgot *n* world, universe, earth
জগাখিচুড়ি jɔgakhicuṛi *n* hodge-podge
জঙ্গল jɔnggol *n* forest, jungle
জটিল joṭil *adj* complex, intricate
জড়ানো jɔṛano *vb* embrace, hug, involve

জন jɔn *n* person, individual
জনপ্রিয় jɔnopriyo *adj* favorite, well-liked
জন্তু jontu *n* animal, creature
জন্ম jɔnmo *n* birth, origin
জন্মদিন jɔnmodi:n *n* birthday
জন্য jɔnno, জন্যে jɔnne *pp* for
জবাব jɔbab *n* answer, reply
জমজ, যমজ jɔmoj *n* twin
জমা করা jɔma kɔra *vb* save, collect
জমি jomi *n* land, soil, real estate
জমিদার jomidar *n* land-owner, landlord
জয় jɔy *n* victory, triumph
জয় করা jɔy kɔra *vb* win
জরুরি joruri *adj* urgent, essential
জরুরি অবস্থা joruri ɔbostha *n* emergency
জল jɔl *n* water
জলদি joldi *adv* quickly, hurriedly
জলপাই jɔlpai *n* olive
জলসা jɔlsha *n* concert, musical soiree
জাগা jaga *vb* wake up, rise from sleep
জাগানো jagano *vb* wake someone up, rouse from sleep
জাতি jati *n* nation, species
জাতীয় jatiyo *adj* national
জাদুঘর jadughɔr *n* museum
জানা jana *vb* know, be aware of
জানানো janano *vb* inform, make known
জানালা janala *n* window
জামা jama *n* shirt, blouse, jacket
জায়গা jayga *n* place, space, room
জাল ja:l *n* fishing net
জাহাজ jahaj *n* ship
জিজ্ঞাসা jiggasha *n* question, inquiry
জিনিস jinish *n* thing, substance, article
জিনিসপত্র jinishpɔtro *n* things, goods
জিব ji:b, জিভ ji:bh *n* tongue
জিরা jira *n* cumin

জিরানো jirano *vb* relax, take a rest
জীবজন্তু ji:bjontu *n* animal, living creature
জীবন jibon *n* life, vitality
জীবিত jibito *adj* existent, alive
জুড়ানো juṛano *vb* cool, soothe, calm
জুড়ি juṛi *n* match, equal
জুতা juta, জুতো juto *n* shoes, footwear
জুয়া juwa *n* gambling
জুস jush *n* juice
জেদি jedi *adj* stubborn, obstinate
জেল jel *n* jail, prison
জেলা jela *n* district, division
জেলে jele *n* fisherman
জোড়া joṛa *n* pair, couple
জোর jor *n* strength, force, power
জোর করা jor kɔra *vb* force, coerce
জোরে jore *adv* loudly, forcefully, fast
জ্ঞান gæn *n* knowledge, perception
জ্বর jɔr *n* fever
জ্বালানি jalani *n* firewood, fuel
জ্বালানো jalano *vb* kindle, light; irritate

ঝ jh

ঝগড়া jhɔgṛa *n* quarrel, altercation
ঝড় jhɔṛ *n* storm, tempest
ঝরনা jhɔrna *n* fountain
ঝাঁকানো jhãkano *vb* shake
ঝাড়ু jhaṛu *n* broom, brush
ঝামেলা jhamela *n* trouble, disturbance
ঝুঁকি jhũki *n* risk, peril
ঝুড়ি jhuṛi *n* basket
ঝোল jhol *n* sauce, soup
ঝোলা jhola *vb* hang, swing, dangle

ট ṭ

টক ṭɔk *adj* sour
টমটম ṭɔmṭɔm *n* horse-drawn carriage
টমেটো ṭomeṭo *n* tomato
টয়লেট ṭɔyleṭ *n* toilet
টলা ṭɔla *vb* waver, stagger, totter
টাকা ṭaka *n* money, Bangladesh currency
টাকা দেওয়া ṭaka deowa *vb* pay
টাটকা ṭaṭka *adj* fresh, not stale
টান ṭa:n *n* pull, tug, attraction
টানা ṭana *vb* pull, draw
টিকটিকি ṭikṭiki *n* gecko, house-lizard
টিকা ṭika *n* vaccination
টিকিট ṭikiṭ, টিকেট ṭikeṭ *n* ticket, stamp
টিয়া ṭiya *n* parrot, parakeet
টুপি ṭupi *n* hat, cap
টুল ṭul *n* stool, wooden seat
টেবিল ṭebil *n* table
টের পাওয়া ṭer paowa *vb* feel, be aware of, perceive
টেলিফোন ṭeliphon *n* telephone
ট্রেন ṭren *n* train

ঠ ṭh

ঠকা ṭhɔka *vb* be cheated, be deceived
ঠকানো ṭhɔkano *vb* cheat, deceive
ঠাণ্ডা ṭhanḍa *adj* cold, cool, calm
ঠিক ṭhi:k *adj* correct, right, proper
ঠিকানা ṭhikana *n* address
ঠেলা ṭhæla *vb* push, shove, thrust
ঠেলাগাড়ি ṭhælagaṛi *n* pushcart, hand wagon

ড ḍ

ডজন ḍɔjon *adj* a dozen
ডবল ḍɔbol *adj* double
ডাক ḍa:k *n* call, summons
ডাক ḍa:k *n* mail
ডাকঘর ḍa:kghɔr *n* post-office
ডাকা ḍaka *vb* call
ডাক্তার ḍaktar *n* doctor
ডান ḍa:n *n* right, right side
ডানা ḍana *n* wing
ডাব ḍa:b *n* green coconut
ডাল ḍa:l *n* branch, twig
ডাল ḍa:l *n* lentils, pulses
ডিম ḍi:m *n* egg
ডুমুর ḍumur *n* fig
ডেকচি ḍekci *n* metallic cooking pot
ডোবা ḍoba *vb* sink, drown

ঢ ḍh

ঢাকা ḍhaka *vb* cover, screen, envelop, conceal
ঢালা ḍhala *vb* pour, cast, mold
ঢেউ ḍheu *n* wave, billow, surge
ঢোকা ḍhoka *vb* enter, go into

ত t / ৎ t

তখন tɔkhon *adv, conj* then, at that time
তত tɔto *adv, conj* so much, to that extent
তবু tobu, তবুও tobuo *conj* in spite of, yet, still
তবে tɔbe *conj* then, thereafter, but
তরকারি tɔrkari *n* curry, spicy meat dish
তরমুজ tormuj *n* watermelon
তরুণ torun *adj* young, fresh

তর্ক tɔrko *n* altercation, argument
তলা tɔla *n* floor, storey; foot, base
তা ta: *pr* that, it
তাই tai *conj* therefore, for that reason
তাঁবু tãbu *n* tent
তাক ta:k *n* shelf
তাকানো takano *vb* look at, see, stare, gaze
তাড়া taṛa *n* hurry, rush, urgency
তাড়াতাড়ি taṛataṛi *adv* quickly, hastily
তাৎপর্য tatporyo *n* significance, meaning
তাপ ta:p *n* heat, temperature, warmth, fever
তামাক tamak *n* tobacco
তামাশা tamasha *n* joke, jest, fun
তার ta:r *n* metal string, wire
তারপর tarpɔr *conj* after that, then
তারা tara *n* star
তারিখ tarikh *n* date
তাল ta:l *n* rhythm, beat
তালা tala *n* padlock; floor, story/storey (*of a building*)
তালাক talak *n* divorce, separation
তালিকা talika *n* list, inventory
তাস ta:sh *n* playing cards
তিনি tini *pr* he, she (*honorific*)
তিমি timi *n* whale
তীর ti:r *n* riverbank
তুচ্ছ tuccho *adj* trivial, insignificant
তুচ্ছ করা tuccho kɔra *vb* neglect, ignore
তুফান tuphan *n* storm, tempest
তুমি tumi *pr* you (*singular familiar*)
তুলনা tulona *n* balance, comparison
তুলনা করা tulona kɔra *vb* compare, liken
তুলা tula *n* cotton
তুষার tushar *n* snow, frost, ice
তৃপ্ত tripto *adj* satisfied, pleased
তেমন temon *adj, adv* such, like, so
তেল tel *n* oil, fuel, petrol, flattery

তেলাপোকা telapoka *n* cockroach
তৈরি toiri *adj* ready, prepared
তো to *emp expr* question, doubt, reassurance
তোমরা tomra *pr* you *(plural, familiar)*
তোলা tola *vb* raise, lift, pluck
তোশক toshok *n* mattress

থ th

থলি tholi *n* bag, purse
থাক tha:k *n* tier, layer, shelf
থাকা thaka *vb* stay, be, live, remain
থানা thana *n* police station
থামা thama *vb* stop, cease
থাল tha:l, থালা thala *n* plate, dish
থুথু thuthu *n* spittle, saliva
থেকে theke *pp, conj* from, since, than

দ d

দই doi *n* yogurt
দক্ষ dɔkkho *adj* skilled, expert
দক্ষিণ dokkhin *n* south
দড়ি doṛi *n* rope, string
দয়া dɔya *n* kindness, mercy
দরকার dɔrkar *n* need, necessity
দরখাস্ত dɔrkhasto *n* application
দরজা dɔrja *n* door
দরজি dorji *n* tailor
দাঁড়ানো dãṛano *vb* stand, wait
দাঁত dã:t *n* tooth
দাগ da:g *n* mark, spot, stain
দাদা dada *n* brother (*older*), grandfather (*paternal*)
দান da:n *n* act of giving, offering
দাম da:m *n* price, cost, value
দামি dami *adj* expensive, costly

দায়িত্ব dayitto *n* responsibility, liability
দারুণ darun *adj* great, intense, excessive
দারোয়ান darowan *n* guard, gatekeeper
দালান dalan *n* building
দিক di:k *n* direction
দিগন্ত digonto *n* horizon
দিদি didi *n* sister (*older*)
দিন di:n *n* day
দিয়ে diye *pp* with (*instr*), through
দিশেহারা dishehara *adj* disorientated, confused, lost
দুঃখ dukkho *n* sorrow, sadness, grief
দুঃখিত dukkhito *adj* sorry, woeful, grieved
দুজন dujɔn *n* two people, both
দুটানা duṭana *n* indecision, dilemma
দুধ du:dh *n* milk
দুনিয়া duniya *n* world, universe
দুপুর dupur *n* midday, noon
দুয়েক duyek *adj* one or two, a few
দুর্বল durbɔl *adj* weak, feeble
দুষ্টু dushṭu *adj* naughty, mischievous
দূত du:t *n* messenger, ambassador
দূতাবাস dutabash *n* embassy
দূর du:r *n* distance
দৃশ্য drissho *n* view, scenery
দৃষ্টি drishṭi *n* view, sight, faculty of seeing
দেওয়া deowa *vb* give
দেওয়াল deowal *n* wall
দেখা dækha *vb* see, look, notice
দেখা করা dækha kɔra *vb* meet, visit
দেড় deṛ *adj, num* one and a half
দেরি deri *n* delay
দেশ desh *n* country, state, homeland
দেশী deshi *adj* indigenous, local
দোকান dokan *n* shop, store
দোষ dosh *n* fault, guilt, vice, crime
দোষ দেওয়া dosh deowa *vb* blame, accuse

দৌড় দেওয়া douṛ deowa *vb* run, take off, rush
দ্বীপ di:p *n* island
দ্রুত druto *adj* quick, swift, speedy

ধ dh

ধনিয়া dhoniya, ধনে dhone *n* coriander
ধনী dhoni *adj* rich, wealthy, affluent
ধন্যবাদ dhɔnnobad *n* thanksgiving, thanks
ধরন dhɔron *n* manner, kind, method
ধরা dhɔra *vb* hold, catch, seize
ধরে dhore *pp* during
ধর্ম dhɔrmo *n* religion, doctrine, creed
ধাঁধা dhãdha *n* riddle, puzzle
ধান dha:n *n* paddy; rice
ধার dha:r *n* edge, border, brink; loan
ধার করা dha:r kɔra *vb* borrow
ধার দেওয়া dha:r deowa *vb* lend
ধারণা dharona *n* idea, concept, notion
ধুলা dhula *n* dust
ধূম dhu:m *n* smoke, fume, steam
ধূমপান dhumpan *n* smoking
ধৈর্য dhoirjo *n* patience, endurance, composure
ধোয়া dhowa *vb* wash, cleanse, scrub
ধ্বংস dhɔngsho *n* destruction, ruin, wreckage

ন n

ন- nɔ- *vb* be not
নইলে noile *conj* if not, otherwise
নখ nɔkh *n* fingernail
নগদ nɔgod *n* cash
নজর nɔjor *n* sight, vision, view
নজর রাখা nɔjor rakha *vb* watch, keep an eye on
নড়া nɔṛa *vb* move, stir
নড়াচড়া nɔṛacɔṛa *n* movement

নতুন notun *adj* new
নদী nodi *n* river, stream
নমস্কার nɔmoshkar *n* greeting, salute
নরম nɔrom *adj* soft, gentle, tender
নলকুপ nolkup *n* tube well
নষ্ট nɔshṭo *adj* spoiled, destroyed, rotten
না na: *adv* not, no
নাই, নেই nai *adv* is not (*denoting absence*)
নাক na:k *n* nose; sense of smell
নাকি naki *adv* or not; *expr* question
নাগাল nagal *n* reach, range, touch
নাচ na:c *n* dance
নাচা naca *vb* dance
নাটক naṭok *n* drama, play
নাড়া naṛa *vb* move, set in motion, stir
নানা nana *adj* various, diverse, many
নাপিত napit *n* barber
নাম nam *n* name
নামকরা namkɔra *adj* famous
নামা nama *vb* descend, get down
নামাজ namaj *n* prayer (*Muslim*)
নামানো namano *vb* set off, drop off, unload
নারিকেল narikel *n* coconut
নার্স nars *n* nurse
নালিশ nalish *n* complaint, accusation
নাস্তা nasta *n* breakfast
নিঃশ্বাস nisshash *n* breath, breathing
নিখুঁত nikhut *adj* perfect, flawless
নিচু nicu *adj* low, down
নিচে nice *pp* below, underneath
নিজ nij *pr* own, self
নিজে nije *pr* oneself
নিন্দা ninda *n* blame, discredit
নিন্দা করা ninda kɔra *vb* blame, reproach
নিয়তি niyoti *n* order, rule, fate
নিয়ন্ত্রণ niyontron *n* control, restraint

নিয়ম niyom *n* system, rule, custom
নিরাপত্তা nirapɔtta *n* security, safety
নিরাপদ nirapɔd *adj* safe, secure
নিরামিষ niramish *adj* vegetarian
নির্দিষ্ট nirdishṭo *adj* determined, fixed
নির্ভর nirbhor *n* support, reliance
নির্ভর করা nirbhor kɔra *vb* rely on, depend on
নিশ্চয় nishcɔy *adj* certain, convinced, sure
নিশ্চিত nishcito *adj* convinced, certain, sure
নিষেধ nishedh *n* prohibition, ban
নিষ্ঠুর nisṭhur *adj* cruel, heartless
নীল ni:l *adj* blue
নুন nu:n *n* salt
নুপুর nupur *n* ankle-bells
নেই nei *vb* is not (*denotes absence*)
নেংটা nængṭa *adj* naked, unclothed
নেতা neta *n* leader, director
নেপালি nepali *adj* Nepali, Nepalese
নেশা nesha *n* intoxication, inebriation
নৌকা nouka *n* boat
ন্যায় næy *n* justice, reasoning, logic

প p

পকেট pɔkeṭ *n* pocket
পক্ষে pɔkkhe *pp* for, on behalf of
পঙ্গু pongu *adj* lame, crippled
পচা pɔca *adj* rotten, spoiled
পছন্দ pɔchondo *n* choice, liking, selection
পড়া pɔṛa *vb* fall, drop
পড়া pɔṛa *vb* read, study
পড়ানো pɔṛano *vb* teach, instruct
পড়াশোনা pɔṛashona *n* study, education
পণ্ডিত ponḍito *adj* learned, erudite, wise
পত্রিকা potrika *n* journal, magazine
পথ pɔth *n* path, way, course

পদ pɔd *n* foot; pace; verse
পয়সা pɔysha *n* money, 0.01 Taka
পর pɔr *adj* other, different, later
পর pɔr, পরে pɔre *pp, adv* after, later, then
পরটা pɔroṭa *n* thin fried bread
পরদা pɔrda *n* screen, curtain, veil
পরপর pɔrpɔr *adv* successively, consecutively
পরম pɔrom *adj* first, supreme
পরশু porshu *n* day after tomorrow
পরা pɔra *vb* wear, put on
পরিকল্পনা porikɔlpona *n* planning
পরিচয় poricɔy *n* acquaintance
পরিচালনা poricalona *n* management, administration
পরিচিত poricito *adj* acquainted, familiar, known
পরিপাটি poripaṭi *adj* tidy, orderly
পরিবর্তন poriborton *n* change, alteration
পরিবর্তে poriborte *pp* instead of, in place of
পরিবহণ poribɔhon *n* transport
পরিবার poribar *n* family
পরিবেশ poribesh *n* surroundings, environment
পরিমাণ poriman *n* amount, quantity
পরিষ্কার porishkar *adj* clean, tidy, neat
পরীক্ষা porikkha *n* examination, test, trial
পরে pɔre *pp, adv* after, afterwards, then, later
পর্যন্ত porjonto *pp, adv* until, as long as, even
পশু poshu *n* animal, beast
পশ্চিম poshcim *n* west
পা pa: *n* leg; foot
পাউডার pauḍar *n* powder
পাউরুটি pauruṭi *n* bread, European bread
পাওনা paona *n* earnings, income; claim
পাওয়া paowa *vb* receive, get, obtain
পাকা paka *vb* ripen, mature
পাকা paka *adj* ripe, mature; permanent
পাকাপাকি করা pakapaki kɔra *vb* finalize, settle
পাখা pakha *n* wing, fan, sail

পাখি pakhi *n* bird
পাগল pagol *adj* mad, crazy, insane
পাছা pacha *n* hip, loins, buttocks
পাজি paji *adj* mischievous, naughty
পাট pa:ṭ *n* jute
পাটি paṭi *n* mat
পাঠানো paṭhano *vb* send, dispatch
পাড় pa:ṛ *n* bank, shore; margin
পাড়া paṛa *n* small habitation, village
পাতলা patla *adj* thin, slender, fine
পাতা pata *n* leaf, page; lid; *vb* spread, lay out, prepare
পাতাল রেল patal rel *n* underground train, subway
পাত্র patro *n* vessel, pot; partner
পাথর pathor *n* stone, rock
পান pa:n *n* betel leaf; act of drinking
পান pa:n *n* act of drinking
পানি pani *n* water
পাপ pa:p *n* sin, lapse, vice
পায়খানা paykhana *n* lavatory, latrine; feces
পার pa:r *n* bank, shore, border
পার হওয়া pa:r hɔowa *vb* cross, pass over
পারা para *vb* be able to, can, may
পার্থক্য parthokko *n* difference, distinction
পালানো palano *vb* flee, run away
পাশ pa:sh *n* side, flank, edge
পাশাপাশি pashapashi *adj* alongside, next to
পাশে pashe *pp* next to, near, alongside
পাস pa:sh *n* pass, permission
পাস করা pa:sh kɔra *vb* pass an examination
পাহাড় pahaṛ *n* mountain, hill, rock
পিঁপড়া pĩpṛa *n* ant
পিছনে pichone *pp* at the back, behind
পিছল pichol, পিছলা pichla *adj* slippery, treacherous
পিঠা piṭha *n* cake, sweet pie
পিতা pita *n* father
পিপাসা pipasha *n* thirst, eager desire

পিয়াজ piyaj (*also* পেঁয়াজ pẽyaj) *n* onion
পুকুর pukur *n* lake, pond
পুড়া puṛa *vb* burn, be scorched
পুতুল putul *n* doll
পুত্র putro *n* son
পুরা pura *vb* fill, stuff, cram; *adj* entire, whole, complete
পুরানো purano *vb* fill, fulfil, satisfy; *adj* old, ancient
পুরুষ purush *n* man, male, person
পুলিশ pulish *n* police
পূর্ণ purno *adj* full, complete, all
পূর্ণিমা purnima *n* full moon
পূর্ব purbo *n* east; first, former
পূর্বে purbe *adv* formerly, previous
পৃথিবী prithibi *n* earth
পেঁচানো pẽcano *vb* twist, involve, entangle
পেঁপে pẽpe *n* papaya
পেঁয়াজ pẽyaj *n* onion
পেচ্ছাব pecchab *n* urine
পেট peṭ *n* stomach
পেনসিল pensil *n* pencil
পেয়ারা peyara *n* guava
পেরেক perek *n* nail, pin, spike
পেশা pesha *n* profession, trade
পোকা poka *n* insect, worm, creepy-crawly
পোয়া powa *n* a quarter, a fourth
পোলাও polao *n* special rice dish, *pilau*
পোশাক poshak *n* dress, garment
পৌঁছা põcha, পৌঁছানো põchano *vb* arrive, reach, come
প্যান্ট pænṭ *n* trousers, pants
প্রকল্প prokɔlpo *n* plan, hypothesis, project
প্রকার prokar *n* kind, type, sort
প্রকাশ prokash *n* revelation, publication
প্রচুর procur *adj* plentiful, abundant, profuse
প্রজাপতি projapoti *n* butterfly
প্রতি proti *pp* towards, regarding
প্রতিদিন protidin *adv* daily, every day

প্রতিবাদ protibad *n* protest, counter-plea
প্রতিরোধ protirodh *n* prevention, resistance
প্রতিশোধ protishodh *n* revenge
প্রতীক protik *n* symbol, sign
প্রত্যেক prottek *adj* each, every
প্রথম prothom *adj* first, chief
প্রধান prodhan *adj* main, chief, principal
প্রধানত prodhanɔto *adv* mainly, above all
প্রভু probhu *n* lord, master, god
প্রমাণ proman *n* proof, evidence
প্রয়োজন proyojɔn *n* necessity, need, purpose
প্রয়োজনীয় proyojoniyo *adj* necessary, essential
প্রশংসা proshɔngsha *n* praise, admiration
প্রশ্ন proshno *n* question
প্রস্তাব prostab *n* proposal
প্রস্তুত prostut *adj* ready, prepared
প্রাণ pran *n* life, life-breath
প্রায় pray *adv* usually, often; almost; resembling, like
প্রার্থনা prarthona *n* prayer, supplication
প্রিয় priyo *adj* dear, beloved, favorite
প্রেম prem *n* love, affection, devotion

ফ ph

ফরসা phɔrsha *adj* fair-complexioned, light-skinned
ফল phɔl *n* fruit, result, effect
ফসল phɔshol *n* harvest
ফাঁক phã:k *n* gap, chink, fissure
ফাঁকি phãki *n* deception, evasion, hoodwinking
ফাটা phaṭa *vb* crack, split, burst, explode
ফিতা phita *n* tape, ribbon
ফিরা phira, ফেরা phera *vb* return, come back
ফুঁ phu: *n* whiff, blow, puff
ফুঁ দেওয়া phu: deoya *vb* blow out, blow
ফুটা phuṭa *vb* bloom, blossom, appear
ফুর্তি phurti *n* enjoyment, merrymaking

ফুল phu:l *n* flower, blossom
ফুলকপি phulkopi *n* cauliflower
ফুসফুস phushphush *n* lungs
ফেরা phera *vb* return, come back
ফেরি pheri *n* ferry
ফেরিওয়ালা pheriowala *n* peddler, hawker
ফেল করা phel kɔra *vb* fail
ফেলা phæla *vb* throw, fling
ফোটা phoṭa *vb* bloom, blossom
ফ্ল্যাট phlæṭ *n* flat, apartment

ব b

বই boi *n* book
বই কি boi ki *adv* of course, naturally
বকশিশ bokshish *n* alms; bakhsheesh
বকা bɔka *vb* scold, tell off
বছর bɔchor *n* year
বটে bɔṭe *adv* just so, true, indeed
বড় bɔṛo *adj* big, large
বড়দিন bɔṛodin *n* Christmas
বদলে bɔdole *pp* instead of, in place of
বন bon *n* forest, wood, jungle
বন্দর bɔndor *n* port, harbor
বন্দুক bonduk *n* gun, musket, rifle
বন্ধ bɔndho *n* tie, bond; bandage; *adj* shut, closed
বন্ধ করা bɔndho kɔra *vb* close, shut, stop
বন্ধু bondhu *n* friend
বন্যা bɔnna *n* flood, deluge
বমি করা bomi kɔra *vb* vomit, be sick
বয়স bɔyosh *n* age
বয়স্ক bɔyoshko *adj* adult, middle-aged
বয়াম bɔyam *n* jar
বরং bɔrong *adv* rather, in preference
বরফ bɔroph *n* ice
বরবটী bɔrboṭi *n* green beans

বর্ণ bɔrno *n* color; letter of the alphabet
বর্ণনা bɔrnona *n* description
বর্ষা bɔrsha *n* rain, rainfall, monsoon
বল bɔl *n* ball; strength
বলা bɔla *vb* speak, talk, say
বলে bole *conj* because of, as, on account of
বসন্ত bɔshonto *n* spring, springtime
বসা bɔsha *vb* sit
বহু bohu *adj* many, numerous
বা ba: *conj, adv* or, instead, whether
বাইরে baire *n, pp* outside, beyond
বাঁ bã: *adj, n* left, the left side
বাঁকা bãka *vb* bend; *adj* bent
বাঁচা bãca *vb* live, survive, be alive
বাঁচানো bãcano *vb* save, rescue, revive
বাঁধা bãdha *vb* tie, fasten; obstruct
বাঁশ bãsh *n* bamboo
বাঁশি bãshi *n* flute, pipe
বাকি baki *adj* remaining, outstanding
বাক্স baksho *n* box, chest, case
বাগান bagan *n* garden
বাঘ ba:gh *n* tiger
বাঙালি bangali *n, adj* Bengali
বাচ্চা bacca *n* child, baby
বাজা baja *vb* ring, strike (*clock*)
বাজানো bajano *vb* play (*a musical instrument*), strike
বাজার bajar *n* market, bazaar
বাজে baje *adj* trashy, cheap, paltry
বাড়তি barṭi *n* excess, surplus; *adj* extra
বাড়া baṛa *vb* grow, increase, develop
বাড়ি baṛi *n* home, residence, village home
বাতাস batash *n* wind, air, breeze
বাতি bati *n* lamp, light, candle
বাতিল batil *adj* cancelled, rejected
বাদ ba:d *n* exception, exclusion, omission
বাদাম badam *n* nut, peanut

বাদামি badami *adj* brown, almond-colored
বাধা badha *n* obstacle, hindrance, impediment
বানর banor *n* monkey, ape
বানানো banano *vb* make, prepare
বাবা baba *n* father
বাবুর্চি baburci *n* cook, chef
বাম bam *adj* left, left-hand
বার ba:r *n* day; fixed time
বালতি balti *n* bucket
বালি bali *n* sand, gravel
বালিশ balish *n* pillow, cushion
বাস bas *n* bus
বাস bash *n* habitation, settlement
বাসা basha *n* house
বাস্তব bastob *adj* true, actual, real
বাস্তবতা bastobota *n* reality
বিকল্প bikɔlpo *n* substitute, alternative
বিকাল bikal *n* afternoon
বিক্রি bikri *n* selling, sale
বিচার bicar *n* judgement, verdict, verification
বিচি bici *n* seed, stone
বিচিত্র bicitro *adj* varied; colorful
বিছানা bichana *n* bed
বিজয় bijɔy *n* victory, triumph, conquest
বিজ্ঞান biggan *n* science
বিজ্ঞাপন biggapon *n* notice, advertisement
বিড়াল biṛal *n* cat
বিড়ি biṛi *n* biri, indigenous cigarette
বিদায় biday *n* farewell, leave-taking
বিদেশ bidesh *n* foreign country, abroad
বিদেশি bideshi *adj* foreign, alien
বিদ্যালয় biddalɔy *n* school, academy
বিদ্যুৎ biddut *n* electricity; lightning
বিধবা bidhoba *n* widow
বিনা bina *pp* without, except
বিন্দু bindu *n* drop

বিপজ্জনক bipɔjjɔnok *adj* dangerous
বিপদ bipɔd *n* danger, hazard
বিবেচক bibecok *adj* thoughtful, judicious
বিবেচনা bibecona *n* consideration, judgment
বিভাগ bibhag *n* division, distribution
বিমান biman *n* aircraft, airplane
বিমানবন্দর bimanbɔndor *n* airport
বিরক্ত birɔkto *adj* annoyed, angry, vexed
বিরহ birɔho *n* parting, separation
বিরুদ্ধে biruddhe *pp* against, in opposition to
বিল bi:l *n* marsh, flood plain
বিলাত bilat *n* foreign country, Europe, England
বিলাতি bilati *adj* foreign
বিলাস bilash *n* luxury, indulgence
বিশেষ bishesh *n* kind, sort, type
বিশেষ bishesh *adj* special, particular
বিশ্বাস bisshash *n* belief, trust, faith
বিশ্বাসী bisshashi *adj* trustworthy, loyal, faithful
বিশ্রাম bisram *n* rest, repose, break
বিশ্রী bisri *adj* ugly, hideous, monstrous
বিশ্লেষণ bisleshon *n* analysis; dissolution
বিষ bi:sh *n* poison, venom
বিষণ্ণ bishɔnno *adj* sad, dejected, despondent
বিষয় bishɔy *n* subject, topic
বুক bu:k *n* chest
বুড়া buṛa *adj* old, elderly (*for people*)
বুড়ি buṛi *n* old woman
বুদ্ধি buddhi *n* wisdom, reason, understanding
বুধবার budhbar *n* Wednesday
বুলানো bulano *vb* caress, pass (*hand*) lightly over
বৃষ্টি brishṭi *n* rain
বৃহস্পতিবার brihɔshpotibar *n* Thursday
বেগুন begun *n* eggplant
বেগুনি beguni *adj* violet, purple
বেচা bæca *vb* sell
বেড়ানো bæṛano *vb* walk, go out, visit

বেতন beton *n* salary, wages
বেতার betar *n* radio
বেপার bæpar *n* trade
বেলা bæla *n* hour, time of day
বেশ besh *adj, adv* quite, nice, fine
বেশি beshi *adj* much, too much, many
বোকা boka *adj* foolish, stupid
বোকামি bokami *n* foolishness, stupidity
বোঝা bojha *vb* understand
বোঝানো bojhano *vb* explain, comfort
বোতল botol *n* bottle
বোতাম botam *n* button
বোধ bodh *n* understanding, consciousness
বোধ হয় bodh hɔy *adv* perhaps
বোন bon *n* sister
বোনা bona *vb* sow, weave, knit
বোবা boba *adj* dumb, speechless, mute
বোমা boma *n* bomb
ব্যক্তি bekti *n* person, man
ব্যক্তিগত bektigɔto *adj* private, personal
ব্যথা bætha *n* pain, ache
ব্যবসা bæbsha *n* business, trade, commerce
ব্যবস্থা bæbostha *n* arrangement, preparation
ব্যবহার bæbohar *n* behavior, use
ব্যর্থ bærtho *adj* futile, vain, useless
ব্যস্ত bæsto *adj* busy, eager, anxious
ব্যাংক bænk *n* bank
ব্যাকরণ bækoron *n* grammar
ব্যাপার bæpar *n* matter, affair; trade
ব্রিজ brij *n* bridge

ভ bh

ভদ্র bhɔdro *adj* gentle, polite, mannerly
ভদ্রলোক bhɔdrolok *n* gentleman
ভয় bhɔy *n* fear, dread, terror

ভরা bhɔra *vb* be filled, be loaded
ভরানো bhɔrano *vb* fill, fill up, load
ভর্তি bhorti *adj* filled, enrolled, replete
ভাই bhai *n* brother (*younger*)
ভাংতি bhangti *n* small coins, change
ভাগ bha:g *n* partition, division
ভাগ্য bhaggo *n* fortune, luck
ভাঙা bhanga *vb* break, crumble, fracture
ভাজা bhaja *vb* fry; roast
ভাড়া bhaṛa *n* rent, hire, fare
ভাত bha:t *n* cooked rice
ভাবা bhaba *vb* think, worry, contemplate
ভার bha:r *n* weight, gravity, burden, pressure
ভারত bharot *n* India
ভাল, ভালো bhalo *adj* good, excellent, nice
ভালবাসা bhalobasha *n* love, affection
ভাষা bhasha *n* language, speech
ভিক্ষা করা bhikkha kɔra *vb* beg, collect alms
ভিজা bhija (*also* ভেজা bheja) *adj* wet, soaked
ভিড় bhiṛ *n* crowd, throng
ভিতর bhitor *n* inside, interior
ভিন্ন bhinno *adj* other, different, separate
ভিসা bhisha *n* visa
ভুল bhu:l *n* mistake, error, omission
ভূত bhu:t *n* ghost, spirit
ভূমি bhumi *n* earth, land, soil
ভূমিকম্প bhumikɔmpo *n* earthquake
ভেড়া bhæṛa *n* sheep, ram
ভোট bhoṭ *n* vote, election
ভোর bhor *n* dawn, daybreak
ভোলা bhola *vb* forget
ভ্রমণ bhromon *n* travel, journey

ম m

মঙ্গল mɔnggol *n* benefit, welfare, good
মঙ্গলবার monggolbar *n* Tuesday
মজা mɔja *n* pleasure, fun, enjoyment
মত mɔt *n* view, opinion
মত mɔto *pp* like, as, according to
মদ mɔd *n* alcohol, wine, spirits
মধু modhu *n* honey
মধ্যে mɔddhe *pp* in between, within
মন mon *n* heart, mind, thought, feeling
মন দেওয়া mon deowa *vb* concentrate
মনে করা mone kɔra *vb* think, consider
মনে পড়া mone pɔṛa *vb* recollect, have on one's mind
মনে রাখা mone rakha *vb* remember, keep in mind
মন-মরা mon-mɔra *adj* disheartened, melancholy, sad
মনস্তত্ত্ব monostɔtto *n* psychology
মনোভাব monobhab *n* attitude, disposition
মনোযোগ monojog *n* attention, concentration
মন্ত্রী montri *n* minister
মন্দ mɔndo *adj* bad, evil, wicked
মন্দির mondir *n* temple, house of worship
ময়দা mɔyda *n* flour
ময়লা mɔyla *n* refuse, litter; *adj* dirty
মরা mɔra *vb* die, pass away
মরিচ moric *n* pepper, chili
মরুভূমি morubhumi *n* desert
মলম mɔlom *n* ointment, balm
মশলা, মসলা mɔshla *n* spice, seasoning
মশা mɔsha *n* mosquito
মশারি mɔshari *n* mosquito net
মসজিদ moshjid *n* mosque
মহিলা mohila *n* woman, lady
মহিষ mohish *n* water buffalo
মা ma *n* mother

মাংস mangsho *n* meat
মাকড়সা makoṛsha *n* spider
মাখন makhon *n* butter
মাছ ma:ch *n* fish
মাছি machi *n* fly
মাজা maja *vb* scour, scrub, cleanse
মাঝে majhe *pp* in between, in the middle
মাটি maṭi *n* earth, clay, soil, ground
মাঠ ma:ṭh *n* field, open land
মাত্র matro *adv* only, merely, just
মাথা matha *n* head, top, summit
মাথা খারাপ matha kharap *adj* crazy, mad
মাথা ব্যথা matha bætha *n* headache
মানা mana *vb* honor, respect; observe
মনিব্যাগ monibæg *n* purse, wallet
মানুষ manush *n* human being, person
মানে mane *n* meaning, import
মাপ ma:p *n* pardon, excuse; measure, dimension
মাফ ma:ph *n* pardon, excuse
মায়া maya *n* illusion, compassion
মারা mara *vb* hit, strike, kill
মারামারি maramari *n* scuffle, fight, affray
মার্কিন markin *adj* American
মাল ma:l *n* merchandise, wares
মালপত্র ma:lpɔtro *n* baggage, luggage
মালা mala *n* garland, necklace
মালিক malik *n* owner, proprietor
মাস ma:sh *n* month
মিথ্যা mittha *n* lie, untruth
মিথ্যা কথা mittha kɔtha *n* lie, falsehood
মিলন milon *n* unity, coming together, meeting
মিলন করা milon kɔra *vb* unite; have sexual intercourse
মিলামিশা milamisha *n* intimate association, familiarity
মিশা misha (*also* মেশা mesha) *vb* mix
মিশুক mishuk *adj* sociable, friendly
মিষ্টি mishṭi *n* sweetmeat; *n, adj* sweet

মিস্ত্রি mistri *n* carpenter, mechanic
মীমাংসা mimangsha *n* solution, reconciliation
মুক্ত mukto *adj* free, liberated
মুক্তি mukti *n* freedom, liberation
মুখ mu:kh *n* face
মুছা mucha (*also* মোছা mocha) *vb* wipe, mop, swab
মুড়ি muṛi *n* parched rice; snack
মুরগি murgi *n* chicken, hen
মুশকিল mushkil *n* problem, difficulty
মুসলমান musholman *n* Muslim
মুহূর্ত muhurto *n* moment, point in time
মূর্খ murkho *adj* foolish, stupid, ignorant
মূল mu:l *n* root, bulb
মূল্য mullo *n* value, worth, cost
মৃত mrito *adj* dead, deceased, lifeless
মেকি meki *adj* counterfeit, fake
মেঘ megh *n* cloud
মেঘলা meghla *adj* cloudy, overcast
মেজাজ mejaj *n* temperament, mood
মেজে meje, মেঝে mejhe *n* floor
মেয়ে meye *n* girl, daughter
মেরামত meramot *n* repair, mending
মেরুদণ্ড merudɔnḍo *n* spine, backbone
মেলা mæla *adj* manifold, plenty, numerous; *n* fair
মেহমান mehoman *n* guest
মোজা moja *n* socks
মোট moṭ *n* total, sum total
মোটা moṭa *adj* fat, corpulent, bulky
মোটামুটি moṭamuṭi *adv* more or less, roughly
মোড়া moṛa *n* wicker stool; *vb* wrap
মোম mom *n* wax, beeswax
মোমবাতি mombati *n* candle
মৌমাছি moumachi *n* bee, honeybee

য j

যখন jɔkhon *conj* when
যত jɔto *conj* as much as, until
যতক্ষণ jɔtokkhɔn *conj* as long as
যত্ন jɔtno *n* care, attention
যথেষ্ট jɔtheshṭo *adj* sufficient, enough
যদি jodi *conj* if, in case
যন্ত্র jɔntro *n* device, tool, instrument
যন্ত্রণা jɔntrona *n* pain, torture
যা ja *pr* that
যাওয়া jaowa *vb* go, move, proceed, advance, leave
যাত্রা jatra *n* journey
যাত্রী jatri *n* passenger
যুক্তি jukti *n* reason, logic
যুদ্ধ juddho *n* war, fight, battle
যে je: *pr* that, which, the one who; *conj* that
যেন jæno *conj* so that
যেমন jæmon *adv* as, like, for instance
যেহেতু jehetu *conj* because, since, as
যোগ jog *n* union, connection
যোগাযোগ jogajog *n* communication, contact
যোগ্য joggo *adj* suitable, worthy, fit, deserving

র r

রওনা rɔona *n* departure, setting off
রকম rɔkom *n* sort, kind, manner, variety
রক্ত rɔkto *n* blood
রক্ষা rɔkkha *n* protection, defense; preservation
রঙ rɔng *n* color, hue, dye, paint
রবিবার robibar *n* Sunday
রস rɔsh *n* juice, liquid; flavor
রসুন roshun *n* garlic
রাখা rakha *vb* place, put, keep

রাগ ra:g *n* anger, passion, rage
রাজধানী rajdhani *n* capital, capital city
রাজনীতি rajniti *n* politics
রাজা raja *n* king
রাজি raji *adj* in agreement, consenting
রাত, রাত্রি ra:t *n* night, nighttime
রানী rani *n* queen
রান্না করা ranna kɔra *vb* cook
রান্নাঘর rannaghɔr *n* kitchen
রামধনু ramdhonu *n* rainbow
রাস্তা rasta *n* road, way
রিকশা riksha *n* rickshaw
রীতি riti *n* method, mode, custom, rule
রীতিমত ritimɔto *adv* regularly, properly
রুটি ruṭi *n* bread
রুপা rupa *n* silver
রুমাল rumal *n* handkerchief
রেখা rekha *n* line, row, stripe
রেলগাড়ি relgaṛi *n* train
রেশম reshom *n* silk
রোগ rog *n* illness, disease
রোজ roj *adj* daily, everyday
রোজা roja *n* fasting, fasting during Ramadan
রোদ rod *n* sun; sunshine

ল।

লক্ষ্য lɔkkho *n* target, aim
লক্ষ্য করা lɔkkho kɔra *vb* notice, observe, intend, aim at
লজ্জা lɔjja *n* embarrassment, shame, diffidence
লবণ lɔbon *n* salt
লম্বা lɔmba *adj* long, tall, lengthy
লাগা laga *vb* begin, start; feel, need
লাগানো lagano *vb* plant; attach; employ
লাঠি laṭhi *n* stick, staff
লাথি lathi *n* kick

লাফ la:ph *n* leap, jump, skip
লাভ la:bh *n* profit, gain, income
লাল la:l *adj* red
লুকানো lukano *vb* hide, put out of sight
লুঙ্গি lungi *n* long loincloth
লেখা lekha *vb* write
লেখাপড়া lekhapɔṛa *n* study, education
লেপ le:p *n* quilt
লেবু lebu *n* lemon
লোক lok *n* person, human being
লোকসান lokshan *n* loss, harm, damage
লোভ lobh *n* greed
লোম lom *n* body hair, fur
লোহা loha *n* iron

শ s/sh

শক্ত shɔkto *adj* strong, firm, hard
শক্তি shokti *n* power, strength, vigor
শখ shɔkh *n* inclination, fancy; hobby
শতাব্দ shɔtabdo, শতাব্দী shotabdi *n* century
শত্রু shotru *n* enemy, opponent
শপথ shɔpɔth *n* oath
শব্দ shɔbdo *n* sound, word, noise
শরম shɔrom *n* shame; modesty
শরীর shorir *n* body; physique
শসা shɔsha *n* cucumber
শহর shɔhor *n* town, city
শাক sha:k *n* spinach
শাকসবজি sha:kshobji *n* green vegetables
শাড়ি shaṛi *n* saree
শান্ত shanto *adj* peaceful, quiet
শান্তি shanti *n* peace
শার্ট sharṭ *n* shirt
শাল sha:l *n* shawl
শিক্ষক shikkhok *n* teacher

শিক্ষিত shikkhito *adj* educated
শিগগির shiggir *adj* quick, fast
শিয়াল shiyal *n* fox; jackal
শিলাবৃষ্টি shilabriishṭi *n* hailstorm
শিল্প shilpo *n* craft, artistry, art
শিল্পী shilpi *n* artist
শিশির shishir *n* dew, frost
শিশু shishu *n* small infant, baby
শীত shi:t *n, adj* cold, chill
শীতকাল shi:tkal *n* winter
শুকনা shukna *adj* dry
শুধু shudhu *adv* only; *adj* empty
শুরু shuru *n* beginning, start
শূকর shukor *n* pig
শূন্য shunno *n* zero, empty, void
শৃঙ্খলা sringkhɔla *n* discipline, control
শেখা shekha *vb* learn, study
শেখানো shekhano *vb* teach
শেষ shesh *n* end, termination
শেষে sheshe *adv* finally, ultimately
শোক shok *n* mourning, grief
শোধ shodh *n* repayment, compensation
শোধ করা shodh kɔra *vb* repay, pay back
শোনা shona *vb* hear, listen
শোনানো shonano *vb* cause to hear, tell
শোয়া showa *vb* lie down
শ্বাস shash *n* breath
শ্বাস নেওয়া shash neowa *vb* breathe
শ্রেণী sreni *n* class, line, range, series
শ্রেষ্ঠ sreshṭho *adj* greatest, best

স sh

সই shoi *n* signature
সওয়া shɔowa *n* one and a quarter
সংখ্যা shɔngkha *n* number, numeral

সংবাদ shɔngbad *n* news, information
সংসদ shɔngshɔd *n* parliament, assembly
সংসার shɔngshar *n* world; family
সংস্কৃত shɔngskrito *n* Sanskrit
সংস্কৃতি shɔngskriti *n* culture
সংস্থা shɔngstha *n* organization, society
সকল shɔkol *adj* entire, whole, all
সকাল shɔkal *n* morning
সঙ্গীত shonggit *n* music, song
সঙ্গে shɔngge *pp* with
সঠিক shoṭhik *adj* correct, accurate
সৎ shɔt *adj* honest, virtuous, good
সতর্ক shɔtɔrko *adj* careful, cautious
সত্ত্ব shɔtto *n* existence, essence, nature, energy
সত্ত্বেও shɔtteo *pp* despite, in spite of
সত্যি shotti *adj* true, actual
সন্তান shɔntan *n* offspring, son/daughter
সন্তুষ্ট shɔntushṭo *adj* satisfied, content
সন্দেহ shɔndeho *n* doubt, suspicion
সন্ধ্যা shɔndha *n* evening, twilight
সপ্তাহ shɔptaho *n* week
সফল shɔphɔl *adj* fruitful, successful
সব shɔb *adj* all, every, whole
সবজি shobji *n* vegetables
সবাই shɔbai *n* everybody
সবুজ shobuj *adj* green
সমকাম shɔmokam *n* homosexuality
সময় shɔmɔy *n* time
সমর্থন shɔmorthon *n* support, help
সমস্ত shɔmosto *adj* complete, whole, all
সমস্যা shɔmossha *n* problem, dilemma
সমাজ shɔmaj *n* society, community
সমাধান shɔmadhan *n* solution, settlement, conclusion
সমান shɔman *n* even, straight, equal
সমিতি shomiti *n* association, society
সমুদ্র shomudro *n* ocean, sea

সম্পত্তি shɔmpotti *n* property, wealth
সম্পর্ক shɔmporko *n* relationship, connection
সম্পূর্ণ shɔmpurno *adv* completely, wholly
সম্প্রতি shɔmproti *adv* recently, lately
সম্বন্ধে shɔmmɔndhe *pp* concerning, about
সম্ভব shɔmbhɔb *adj* probable, likely
সম্মান shɔmman *n* respect
সরকার shɔrkar *n* government
সর্দি shordi *n* cold, flu
সরল shɔrol *adj* honest, simple, candid
সরা shɔra *vb* move, stir, step aside
সরিষা shorisha *n* mustard
সরু shoru *adj* narrow, delicate, thin
সর্বনাশ shɔrbonash *n* disaster, ruin
সস্তা shɔsta *adj* cheap
সহজ shɔhoj *adj* easy, simple, innate
সহ্য shɔjjo *n* tolerance, endurance
সাইকেল saikel *n* bicycle
সাইজ saij *n* size
সাংবাদিক shangbadik *n* journalist
সাঁতার shãtar *n* swimming
সাগর shagor *n* sea, ocean
সাজা shaja *vb* be dressed, be decorated
সাজানো shajano *vb* dress, decorate, embellish, fit out
সাড়ে shaṛe *adj* half past, plus one half
সাদা shada *adj* white
সাধারণ shadharon *adj* usual, ordinary, common
সাধারণত shadharonoto *adv* usually, generally
সাধু shadhu *n* saint
সান্ত্বনা shantona *n* consolation, solace
সাপ sha:p *n* snake
সাবধান shabdhan *adj* cautious, careful
সাবান shaban *n* soap
সামনে shamne *pp* in front of, facing
সামান্য shamanno *adj* little, trifling, insignificant
সারা shara *vb* finish, accomplish, be cured

সারা shara *adj* whole, entire, all
সাহস shahosh *n* courage, boldness, bravery
সাহায্য shahajjo *n* help, assistance, aid, support
সাহিত্য shahitto *n* literature
সাহেব shaheb *n* European gentleman, Sir, Mr.
সিংহ shingho *n* lion
সিঁড়ি shiṛi *n* stairs, staircase
সিগারেট sigareṭ *n* cigarette
সিদ্ধ shiddho *adj* boiled; realized, fulfilled; expert
সিদ্ধ করা shiddho kɔra *vb* boil, cook
সিদ্ধান্ত shiddhanto *n* decision, conclusion
সিনেমা sinema *n* cinema
সীমা shima *n* limit, frontier, periphery
সুখ shu:kh *n* happiness, ease, comfort
সুটকেস sutkes *n* suitcase
সুতরাং shutorang *conj* so, hence, consequently
সুন্দর shundor *adj* beautiful, pleasing, nice, lovely
সুবিধা shubidha *n* advantage, convenience
সুযোগ shujog *n* chance, opportunity
সুর shu:r *n* voice, tone, pitch
সুস্থ shustho *adj* sound, healthy, well
সূর্য shurjo *n* sun
সৃষ্টি srishṭi *n* creation
সে she: *pr* he, she (*ordinary*); that
সেই shei *adj* that, that very
সেবা sheba *n* care, serving, nursing
সেবিকা shebika *n* attendant, nurse (*f*)
সেরা shera *adj* excellent, best
সৈনিক shoinik *n* soldier, fighter
সোজা shoja *adj* straight, honest, upright
সোনা shona *n* gold
স্কুল sku:l *n* school
স্তম্ভিত stombhito *adj* stunned, astonished
স্থান stha:n *n* place, region, locality
স্থাপত্য sthapotto *n* architecture
স্থির sthi:r *adj* calm, still

স্নান sna:n *n* bath, bathing, ablutions
স্নান ঘর sna:n ghɔr *n* bathroom
স্পর্শ spɔrsho *n* touch, contact
স্পষ্ট spɔshṭo *adj* clear, evident, explicit
স্বপ্ন shɔpno *n* dream
স্বভাব shɔbhab *n* nature, characteristic
স্বর্গ shɔrgo *n* heaven, bliss
স্বস্তি shosti *n* comfort, contentment
স্বাদ shad *n* taste, flavor
স্বাধীন shadhin *adj* independent, free
স্বাধীনতা shadhinota *n* independence
স্বাভাবিক shabhabik *adj* natural, usual, normal
স্বার্থ shartho *n* self-interest, egoism
স্বাস্থ্য shastho *n* health, hygiene, happiness
স্বীকার করা shikar kɔra *vb* confess, admit, acquiesce
স্মৃতি sriti *n* memory, recollection
স্রোত srot *n* current, flow of water

হ h

হওয়া hɔowa *vb* be, become, happen, occur
হজম hɔjom *n* digestion
হঠাৎ hɔṭhat *adv* suddenly
হতাশ hɔtash *adj* dejected, crestfallen
হরতাল hɔrtal *n* strike
হলদে hɔlde, হলুদ holud *adj* yellow
হাউমাউ haumau *n* uproar; complaint
হাঁটা hãṭa *vb* walk, go on foot
হাঁটু hãṭu *n* knee
হাঁপানি hãpani *n* asthma
হাঁস hã:sh *n* duck
হাজার hajar *num* thousand
হাজির hajir *adj* present, in attendance
হাট ha:ṭ *n* market
হাত ha:t *n* hand
হাত–খরচ ha:t–khɔroc *n* pocket money

হাতি hati *n* elephant
হারা hara *vb* be defeated, lose
হারানো harano *vb* lose, misplace
হালকা halka *adj* light, easy, mild
হাসা hasha *vb* laugh, smile
হাসি hashi *n* laughter, smile
হিংসা hingsha *n* malice, envy, jealousy
হিন্দু hindu *n* Hindu
হিসাব hishab, হিসেব hisheb *n* accounting, calculation
হৃদয় ridɔy *n* heart; mind
হেমন্ত hemonto *n* autumn
হোটেল hoṭel *n* hotel

ENGLISH – BANGLA DICTIONARY

The English-Bangla entries are given in English alphabetical order. Numbers are given separately at the end of the phrasebook section (pages 210-211).

A

able *adj* সমর্থ shɔmɔrtho, দক্ষ dɔkkho
about *adv* (*approximately*) মোটামুটি moṭamuṭi; *prep* (*concerning*) সম্বন্ধে shɔmmondhe
above *prep* উপর upor
absent *adj* নেই nei
accident *n* একসিডেন্ট eksiḍenṭ, দুর্ঘটনা durghɔtona
account *n* হিসাব hishab
actor *n* অভিনেতা obhineta
actually *adv* আসলে ashole
address *n* ঠিকানা ṭhikana
advice *n* উপদেশ upodesh, পরামর্শ pɔramɔrsho
after *adv, prep* পর pɔr, পরে pɔre
afternoon *n* বিকাল bikal
afterwards *conj* তারপরে tarpɔre
again *adv* আবার abar
against *prep* বিরুদ্ধে biruddhe
age *n* বয়স bɔyosh
agree *vb* রাজি হওয়া raji hɔowa
agriculture *n* চাষ cash, কৃষি krishi
air *n* হাওয়া haowa, বাতাস batash
air-conditioning *n* শীতাতপ নিয়ন্ত্রণ shitatop niyontron, এ সি e si
airplane *n* বিমান biman
airport *n* বিমানবন্দর bimanbɔndor
alcohol *n* মদ mɔd

alike *adj* একি eki
alive *adj* জীবিত jibito
all *adj* সব shɔb, সকল shɔkol, সমস্ত shɔmosto
allergy *n* এলার্জি elarji
allow *vb* অনুমতি দেওয়া onumoti deowa
almost *adv* প্রায় pray
alone *adj* একা æka
already *adv* ইতিমধ্যে itimoddhe
alright *adv* ঠিক আছে ṭhik ace
also *adv* ও o, আরও aro
although *conj* যদিও jodio
always *adv* সব সময় shɔb shɔmɔy, চিরদিন cirodin
amazement *n* অবাক ɔbak
ambassador *n* দূত dut
ambulance *n* অ্যাম্বুলেন্স æmbulens
among *prep* মধ্যে mɔddhe
amusement *n* আমোদ-প্রমোদ amod-promod
and *conj* আর ar, ও o, এবং ebɔng
anger *n* রাগ rag, ক্রোধ krodh
angry *adj* রেগে rege, ক্রুদ্ধ kruddho
animal *n* পশু poshu, জীবজন্তু jibjontu
another *adj* (*additional*) আর একটা ar ækṭa; (*different*) অন্য একটা ɔnno ækṭa
answer *n* উত্তর uttor, জবাব jɔbab
ant *n* পিঁপড়া pĩpṛa
antiseptic *adj* পচন-নিবারক pɔcon-nibarok
anxiety *n* দুশ্চিন্তা dushcinta
anxious *adj* উদ্বিগ্ন udbigno, চিন্তিত cintito
any *adj* যে কোনও je kono
anyone *n* যে কেউ je keu
anything *n* যে কোনও কিছু je kono kicu
apartment *n* ফ্ল্যাট phlæṭ
apologize *vb* দুঃখ প্রকাশ করা dukkho prokash kɔra, ক্ষমা চাওয়া khɔma caowa
apparent *adj* স্পষ্ট spɔshṭo
appear *vb* হাজির হওয়া hajir hɔowa

apple *n* আপেল apel
apply *vb* দরখাস্ত করা dɔrkhasto kɔra
appointment *n* নিয়োগ niyog
appropriate *adj* উপযুক্ত upojukto
approval *n* অনুমোদন onumodon
Arab *n* আরববাসী arobbashi
Arabic *adj* আরবী arobi
archeology *n* প্রত্নবিদ্যা protnobidda
architect *n* স্থপতি sthɔpoti
architecture *n* স্থাপত্য sthapotto
area *n* এলাকা elaka
argue *vb* তর্ক করা tɔrko kɔra
argument *n* তর্ক tɔrko
arm *n* হাত ha:t, বাহু bahu
army *n* বাহিনী bahini, সেনা shena
around *adv* চারদিকে cardike
arrangement *n* ব্যবস্থা bæbostha, বিন্যাস binnash
arrive *vb* পৌঁছানো poũcano
art *n* শিল্প shilpo
article *n* প্রবন্ধ probondho
artificial *adj* কৃত্রিম kritrim
artist *n* শিল্পী shilpi
as *adv, conj* যেমন jæmon
ask *vb* জিজ্ঞাসা করা jiggasha kɔra
ask for *vb* চাওয়া caowa
assistant *n* সহায় shɔhay, সহকারী shɔhokari
association *n* সমিতি shomiti, সংঘ shɔngho
assume *vb* মনে করা mone kɔra, ধারণা করা dharona kɔra
asthma *n* হাঁপানি hãpani
astonished *adj* স্তম্ভিত stombhito
atheist *n* নাস্তিক nastik
at least *adv* অন্তত ɔntoto
atmosphere *n* আবহাওয়া abhaowa
at once *adv* সঙ্গে সঙ্গে shɔngge shɔngge
attach *vb* লাগা laga, লাগানো lagano
attack *n* আক্রমণ akromon, হামলা hamla

attempt *n* চেষ্টা ceshṭa
attend *vb* সেবা করা sheba kɔra
attention *n* মনোযোগ monojog
attitude *n* মনোভাব monobhab
aubergine *n* বেগুন begun
aunt → *see kinship terms (pages 205-207)*
author *n* লেখক lekhok
automatic *adj* এমনি emni, স্বয়ংক্রিয় shɔyongkriyo
avoid *vb* এড়ানো eṛano
awake *vb* জাগা jaga
aware *adj* সতর্ক shɔtɔrko, সচেতন shɔcetɔn
away *adv* দূরে du:re
awful *adj* জঘন্য jɔghonno
awkward *adj* অস্বস্তি ɔshosti
axe *n* কুড়াল kuṛal

B

baby *n* শিশু shishu, বাচ্চা bacca
back *n* পিঠ pi:ṭh
bad *adj* খারাপ kharap
bag *n* থলি tholi
baggage *n* মালপত্র ma:lpɔtro
balance *n* সমতা shɔmota
ball *n* বল bɔ:l
bamboo *n* বাঁশ bã:sh
banana *n* কলা kɔla
bank *n* (*financial institution*) ব্যাংক bænk; (*side of a river*) পাড় paṛ
bar *n* পানশালা panshala
barber *n* নাপিত napit
bare *adj* উলঙ্গ ulɔnggo
barefoot *adj* খালি পায়ে khali paye
bargain *vb* দামাদামি করা damadami kɔra
basic *adj* মৌলিক moulik
basket *n* টুকরি, ঝুড়ি ṭukri, jhuṛi

bath *n* গোসল goshol, স্নান snan
bathe *vb* গোসল করা goshol kɔra
bathroom *n* গোসলখানা gosholkhana, বাথরুম bathrum
battery *n* ব্যাটারি bæṭari
be *vb* (*become*) হওয়া hɔowa; (*exist*) আছ- ac-
beach *n* সমুদ্রতীর shomudrotir
bean *n* শিম si:m, বর্বটি bɔrboṭi
bear *n* ভালুক bhaluk
beard *n* দাড়ি daṛi
beat *vb* মারা mara
beautiful *adj* সুন্দর shundor
because *conj* কারণ karon
become *vb* হওয়া hɔowa
bed *n* বিছানা bicana
bedroom *n* সোবার ঘর shobar ghɔr
bee *n* মৌমাছি moumaci
beef *n* গরুর মাংস gorur mangsho
before *prep* আগে age
beg *vb* ভিক্ষা করা bhikkha kɔra
beggar *n* ভিক্ষুক bhikkhuk
begin *vb* লাগা laga, আরম্ভ করা arɔmbho kɔra
beginning *n* আরম্ভ arɔmbho, শুরু shuru
behind *prep* পিছনে picone
belief *n* বিশ্বাস bisshash
below *prep* নিচে nice
beneath *prep* নিচে nice
benefit *n* লাভ la:bh
besides *adv, conj* তা ছাড়া ta caṛa
best *adj* সেরা shera, শ্রেষ্ঠ sreshṭho
bet *vb* জুয়া খেলা juwa khæla
betel-leaf *n* পান pa:n
better *adj* আরও ভাল aro bhalo
between *prep* মাঝে majhe, মধ্যে moddhe
bicycle *n* সাইকেল saikel
big *adj* বড় bɔṛo
bill *n* টাকার হিসাব ṭakar hishab

bird *n* পাখি pakhi
birth *n* জন্ম jɔnmo
birthday *n* জন্মদিন jɔnmodin
biscuit *n* বিস্কুট biskuṭ
bit *n, adv* টুকরা ṭukra, কিছু kicu, একটু ekṭu
bitter *adj* তেতো teto, তিতা tita
black *adj* কালো kalo
blanket *n* কম্বল kɔmbol
bleed *vb* রক্ত পড়া rɔkto pɔṛa
blessing *n* আশীর্বাদ ashirbad
blind *adj* অন্ধ ɔndho
blood *n* রক্ত rɔkto
blouse *n* ব্লাউজ blauj
blue *adj* নীল ni:l
boat *n* নৌকা nouka, নৌকো nouko
body *n* গা ga:, শরীর shorir
bomb *n* বোমা boma
bone *n* হাড় haṛ, হাড্ডি haḍḍi
book *n* বই boi
boot *n* বুটজুতা buṭjuta
border *n* কিনারা kinara, সীমা shima
bother *vb* জ্বালানো jalano
bottle *n* বোতল botol
boundary *n* সীমানা shimana
box *n* বাক্স baksho
boy *n* ছেলে cele, বালক balok, খোকা khoka
brake *n* ব্রেক brek
brave *adj* সাহসী shahoshi
bread *n* রুটি, চাপাটি ruṭi, capaṭi
break *vb* ভাঙা bhangga, ভাঙানো bhanggano
breakfast *n* নাস্তা nasta
breath *n* নিঃশ্বাস nishash
breathe *vb* নিঃশ্বাস নেওয়া nishash neowa
bribe *n* ঘুষ ghu:sh
brick *n* ইট i:ṭ
bridge *n* পূল, ব্রিজ pu:l, brij

bring *vb* আনা ana
British *adj* ব্রিটিশ briṭish
broken *adj* ভাঙা bhangga
brother *n* ভাই bhai
brown *adj* বাদামি badami
bucket *n* বালতি balti
buffalo *n* মহিষ mohish
bug *n* (*insect*) পোকা poka
build *vb* গড়া gɔṛa, গড়িয়ে তোলা goṛiye tola
building *n* দালান dalan, বাড়ি baṛi
bullet *n* গুলি guli
burglar *n* চোর cor, সিঁধেল চোর shĩdel cor
burn *vb* পুড়া puṛa, পুড়ানো puṛano
bus *n* বাস bas
business *n* ব্যবসা bæbsha
busy *adj* ব্যস্ত bæsto
but *adv, conj* কিন্তু kintu, তবে tɔbe, ছাড়া caṛa
butterfly *n* প্রজাপতি projapoti
buy *vb* কেনা kena

C

cabbage *n* বাঁধাকপি bãdhakopi
café *n* কফিখানা kophikhana
cage *n* খাঁচা khãca
cake *n* পিঠা kek, কেক piṭha
calendar *n* পঞ্জিকা ponjika
call *vb* ডাকা ḍaka
call off *vb* বাতিল করা batil kɔra
calm *adj* শান্ত shanto
camel *n* উট u:ṭ
camera *n* ক্যামেরা kæmera
can *vb* (*be able to*) পারা para
cancel *vb* বাতিল করা batil kɔra
candle *n* মোমবাতি mombati
capital city *n* রাজধানী rajdhani

car *n* গাড়ি gaṛi
care *n* যত্ন jɔtno
careful *adj* সতর্ক shɔtɔrko
carpet *n* গালিচা galica
carrot *n* গাজর gajor
carry *vb* নেওয়া neowa, কোলে নেওয়া kole neowa
cash *n* নগদ টাকা nɔgod ṭaka
cat *n* বিড়াল biṛal, বেড়াল beṛal
catastrophe *n* সর্বনাশ shɔrbonash
catch *vb* ধরা dhɔra
cause *n* কারণ karon
caution *n* সাবধানতা shabdhanota
cave *n* গুহা guha
celebrate *vb* পালন করা palon kɔra
cell phone *n* মোবাইল mobail
center *n* কেন্দ্র kendro, মধ্য mɔddho
central *adj* কেন্দ্রীয় kendriyo, মধ্যে mɔddhe
century *n* শতাব্দ shɔtabdo, শতাব্দী shɔtabdi
certain *adj* নিশ্চিত nishcito
certificate *n* সনদ shɔnod, প্রমাণ পত্র proman potro
chair *n* চেয়ার ceyar
chance *n* সুযোগ shujog
change *n* (*alteration*) পরিবর্তন poriborton; (*loose coins*) *n* খুচরা khucra
charming *adj* মনোরম mɔnorom
chat *vb* গল্প করা gɔlpo kɔra
cheap *adj* সস্তা shɔsta
cheat *vb* ঠকা ṭhɔka, ঠকানো ṭhɔkano
check *n* চেক cek
cheese *n* পনির ponir
chess *n* দাবাখেলা dabakhæla
chest *n* (*front of the body*) বুক bu:k; (*box*) সিন্দুক shinduk
chicken *n* মুর্গি murgi
chief *n* নেতা neta
child *n* বাচ্চা bacca
childhood *n* ছোটবেলা choṭobela

chili *n* কাঁচা মরিচ kãca moric
Chinese *adj* চীনা cina
chocolate *n* চকলেট cɔkleṭ
choice *n* পছন্দ pɔchondo
choose *vb* পছন্দ করা pɔchondo kɔra, বেছে নেওয়া beche neowa
Christian *adj* খ্রিস্টান khrishṭan
church *n* গির্জা girja
chutney *n* আচার acar, চাটনি caṭni
cigarette *n* সিগারেট sigareṭ, বিড়ি biṛi
cinema *n* সিনেমা sinema
cinnamon *n* দারচিনি darcini
circle *n* বৃত্ত britto, পরিধি poridhi
circumstance *n* অবস্থা ɔbostha
circus *n* সার্কাস sarkas
city *n* শহর shɔhor
class *n* (*division in schools*) ক্লাস klash; (*social*) জাতি jati
clean *adj* পরিষ্কার porishkar; *vb* পরিষ্কার করা porishkar kɔra
clear *adj* স্পষ্ট spɔshṭo
clever *adj* চালাক calak
climate *n* আবহাওয়া abhaowa
clock *n* ঘড়ি ghoṛi
close *adj, adv* কাছে kache, কাছাকাছি kachakachi; *vb* বন্ধ করা bɔndho kɔra
cloth *n* কাপড় kapoṛ
clothes *n* পোশাক poshak, কাপড়-চোপড় kapoṛ-copoṛ
cloud *n* মেঘ megh
cock *n* মোরগ morog
cockroach *n* তেলাপোকা telapoka
coconut *n* নারিকেল narikel
coffee *n* কফি kophi
cold *adj* ঠাণ্ডা ṭhanḍa, শীতল shitol
college *n* কলেজ kɔlej
color *n* রঙ rɔng
comb *n* চিরুনি ciruni

come *vb* আসা asha
comfort *n* আরাম aram
command *n* আদেশ adesh, হুকুম hukum
common *adj* সাধারণ shadharon
communist *n* সাম্যবাদী shammobadi
companion *n* সঙ্গী shonggi
company *n* কোম্পানি kompani
compare *vb* তুলনা করা tulona kɔra
complaint *n* অভিযোগ obhijog
complete *adj* সম্পূর্ণ shɔmpurno, পুরা pura, পুরো puro
complicated *adj* জটিল joṭil
computer *n* কম্পিউটার kɔmpiuṭar
conceal *vb* লুকিয়ে রাখা lukiye rakha
condition *n* অবস্থা ɔbostha
conduct *n* আচরণ acoron, ব্যবহার bæbohar
conflict *n* দ্বন্দ্ব dɔndo, বিরোধ birodh
consent *vb* রাজি হওয়া raji hɔowa
consulate *n* দূতাবাস dutabash
contact *n* যোগাযোগ jogajog
continent *n* মহাদেশ mɔhadesh
continue *vb* চালিয়ে যাওয়া caliye jaowa
contraception *n* গর্ভনিরোধ gɔrbhonirodh
convenient *adj* সুবিধাজনক shubidhajɔnok
conversation *n* আলাপ alap, কথাবার্তা kɔthabarta
cook *vb* রান্না করা ranna kɔra; *n* বাবুর্চি baburci
cooker *n* চুলা cula
copy *n* নকল nɔkol, প্রতিমূর্তি protimurti
corn *n* (*grain*) শস্য shɔssho; (*maize*) *n* ভুট্টা bhuṭṭa
correct *adj* ঠিক ṭhi:k, সঠিক shoṭhi:k
corruption *n* ঘুষ ghu:sh, দুর্নীতি durniti
cost *n* (*price*) দাম da:m; (*expense*) খরচ khɔroc
cotton *n* (*raw*) তুলা tula; (*cloth*) সুতি shuti
cough *n* কাশি kashi
count *vb* গোনা gona
country *n* দেশ desh
courage *n* সাহস shahosh

courtyard *n* উঠান uṭhan
cover *vb* ঢাকা ḍhaka
cow *n* গরু goru
crazy *adj* পাগল pagol
create *vb* সৃষ্টি করা srishṭi kɔra
crime *n* অপরাধ ɔporadh
crocodile *n* কুমির kumir
crowd *n* ভিড় bhi:ṛ
crowded *adj* জমজম jɔmjɔm, জনাকীর্ণ jɔnakirno
cry *vb* (*weep*) কাঁদা kãda; (*shout*) চিৎকার করা citkar kɔra, চেঁচামেচি করা cæ̃cameci kɔra
cucumber *n* শসা shɔsha
culture *n* সংস্কৃতি shɔngskriti
cup *n* কাপ kap
cupboard *n* আলমারি almari
curious *adj* উৎসুক utshuk, কৌতূহলী koutuholi
current *n* (*electricity*) বিদ্যুৎ biddut; (*flow*) স্রোত srot; *adj* চলতি colti
curry *n* তরকারি tɔrkari
curse *n* অভিশাপ obhishap
curtain *n* পরদা pɔrda
curve *n* বাঁক bãk, ঘোঁজ ghõj
cushion *n* বালিশ balish
cut *vb* কাটা kaṭa
cyclone *n* ঘূর্ণিঝড় ghurnijhɔṛ

D

daily *adj* রোজ roj, দৈনিক doinik
damage *n* ক্ষতি khoti
dance *n* নাচ nac
danger *n* বিপদ bipɔd
dangerous *adj* বিপজ্জনক bipɔjjɔnok
dark *adj* অন্ধকার ɔndhokar, আঁধার ãdhar
darkness *n* অন্ধকার ɔndhokar
date *n* (*day of the month*) তারিখ tarikh; (*fruit*) *n* খেজুর khejur

daughter *n* মেয়ে meye
dawn *n* ভোর bhor
day *n* দিন di:n
day after tomorrow *n* আগামী পরশু agami porshu
day before yesterday *n* গত পরশু gɔto porshu
dead *adj* মরা mɔra, মৃত mrito
deaf *adj* কালা kala
dear *adj* প্রিয় priyo
death *n* মরণ mɔron, মৃত্যু mrittu
decide *vb* সিদ্ধান্ত করা shiddhanto kɔra
deep *adj* গভীর gobhir
deer *n* হরিণ horin
definite *adj* নিশ্চিত nishcito, যথাযথ jɔthajɔth
delay *n* দেরি deri
deliberate *adj* ইচ্ছা করে iccha kore
democracy *n* গণতন্ত্র gɔnotɔntro
dentist *n* দাঁতের ডাক্তার dãter ḍaktar
deny *vb* অস্বীকার করা ɔsshikar kɔra
depart *vb* রওনা দেওয়া rɔona deowa
department *n* বিভাগ bibhag
departure *n* রওনা rɔona, প্রস্থান prosthan
depend *vb* নির্ভর করা nirbhɔr kɔra
describe *vb* বর্ণনা করা bɔrnona kɔra
desert *n* মরুভূমি morubhumi
desk *n* লেখার টেবিল lekhar ṭebil
despair *n* হতাশা hɔtasha
destiny *n* ভাগ্য bhaggo, নিয়তি niyoti
development *n* অগ্রগতি ɔgrogoti, উন্নতি unnoti
devotion *n* উপাসনা upashɔna, ভক্তি bhokti
diabetes *n* বহুমূত্র রোগ bohumutro rog
dialect *n* উপভাষা upobhasha
diarrhea *n* পাতলা পায়খানা patla paykhana, পেটের অসুখ peṭer ɔshukh
dictionary *n* অভিধান obhidhan
die *vb* মরা mɔra, মরে যাওয়া more jaowa, মারা যাওয়া mara jaowa

difference *n* পার্থক্য parthokko, তফাত tɔphat
different *adj* ভিন্ন bhinno
difficult *adj* কঠিন koṭhin, শক্ত shɔkto
digestion *n* হজম hɔjom, জারণ jaron
dinner *n* রাতের খাবার rater khabar, ভাত bha:t
diplomat *n* দূত du:t
direct *adj, adv* সোজা shoja; *vb* পরিচালনা করা poricalona kɔra
direction *n* দিক di:k
dirty *adj* ময়লা mɔyla, সমল shɔmol
disagreement *n* অমিল ɔmil, মতভেদ mɔtobhed
disaster *n* দুর্ঘটনা durghɔṭona, সর্বনাশ shɔrbonash
discipline *n* নিয়ন্ত্রণ niyontron, শৃঙ্খলা sringkhɔla
discover *vb* আবিষ্কার করা abishkar kɔra
discussion *n* আলোচনা alocɔna
disease *n* রোগ rog
dish *n* বাটি baṭi, থালা thala
dislike *n* অপছন্দ ɔpɔchondo
distance *n* দূর du:r
distant *adj* দূরে du:re
district *n* জেলা jela
disturb *vb* বিরক্ত করা birokto kɔra, জ্বালানো jalano
divorce *n* তালাক talak, বিচ্ছেদ biched
do *vb* করা kɔra
doctor *n* ডাক্তার ḍaktar
dog *n* কুকুর kukur
doll *n* পুতুল putul
donate *vb* দান করা da:n kɔra
donkey *n* গাধা gadha
door *n* দরজা dɔrja
doubt *n* সন্দেহ shɔndeho
down *adv* নিচে nice
dozen *n* ডজন ḍɔjon
drama *n* নাটক naṭok
draw *vb* আঁকা ãka
dream *n* স্বপ্ন shɔpno; *vb* স্বপ্ন দেখা shɔpno dækha

drink *vb* খাওয়া khaowa,পান করা pa:n kɔra; *n* পানীয় paniyo
drive *vb* চালানো calano
drop *vb* পড়ে যাওয়া poṛe jaowa
drug *n* ওষুধ oshudh
drum *n* তবলা tɔbla, ঢোল ḍhol
dry *adj* শুকনা shukna
duck *n* হাঁস hã:sh
during *prep* ধরে dhore
duty *n* কর্তব্য kɔrtobbo
dye *n* রং, রঙ rɔng
dysentry *n* আমাশা amasha

E

each *adj* প্রত্যেক prottek
ear *n* কান ka:n
early *adv* সকালে shɔkale, তাড়াতাড়ি taṛataṛi
earn *vb* কামানো kamano, উপার্জন করা uparjon kɔra
earring *n* কানের ফুল kaner phu:l
earth *n* পৃথিবী prithibi, দুনিয়া duniya
earthquake *n* ভূমিকম্প bhumikɔmpo
east *adj* পূর্ব purbo
easy *adj* সহজ shɔhoj
eat *vb* খাওয়া khaowa
economy *n* অর্থনীতি ɔrthoniti
education *n* শিক্ষা shikkha
effort *n* চেষ্টা ceshṭa, প্রয়াস proyash
egg *n* ডিম ḍi:m
eggplant *n* বেগুন begun
electricity *n* বিদ্যুৎ biddut
elephant *n* হাতি hati
embarrass *vb* লজ্জা দেওয়া lɔjja deowa
embassy *n* দূতাবাস dutabash
emergency *n* জরুরি অবস্থা joruri ɔbostha, বিপদ bipɔd
emotion *n* অনুভূতি onubhuti, আবেগ abeg
employ *vb* কাজে লাগানো kaje lagano

empty *adj* খালি khali
end *n* শেষ shesh, ইতি iti
endure *vb* সহ্য করা shɔjjo kɔra
enemy *n* শত্রু shotru
energy *n* শক্তি shokti
engine *n* ইঞ্জিন injin
English *n* ইংরেজ ingrej; *adj* ইংরেজি ingreji
enjoy *vb* ভাল লাগা bhalo laga, পছন্দ করা pɔchondo kɔra
enough *adv* যথেষ্ট jɔtheshṭo
enter *vb* ঢোকা ḍhoka, প্রবেশ করা probesh kɔra
entertainment *n* আমোদ-প্রমোদ amod-promod
environment *n* পরিবেশ poribesh
envy *n* হিংসা hingsha
equal *adj* সমান shɔman
error *n* ভুল bhu:l
especially *adv* বিশেষভাবে bisheshbhabe
essential *adj* প্রয়োজনীয় proyojoniyo
establish *vb* স্থাপন করা sthapon kɔra
Europe *n* ইউরোপ iurop
European *adj* ইউরোপীয় iuropiyo
even *adv* এমনকি emonki
evening *n* সন্ধ্যা shɔndha
event *n* ঘটনা ghɔṭona
ever *adv* কখনও kɔkhono
every *adj* প্রতি proti, প্রত্যেক prottek
everybody *n* সবাই shɔbai, সকলে shɔkole
everyone *n* সবাই shɔbai, সকলে shɔkole
everything *n* সব কিছু shɔb kichu
everywhere *adv* সব জায়গায় shɔb jaygay, সবখানে shɔbkhane
examination *n* পরীক্ষা porikkha
example *n* উদাহরণ udahɔron
excellent *adj* সেরা shera, চমৎকার cɔmotkar
except *prep* ছাড়া chaṛa, বাদে bade
exchange *n* বিনিময় binimɔy
exercise *n* চর্চা cɔrca

exist *vb* আছ্- ach-, থাকা thaka
expand *vb* বিস্তার করা bistar kɔra
expect *vb* আশা করা asha kɔra
expensive *adj* দামি dami
experience *n* অভিজ্ঞতা obhiggɔta
explain *vb* বোঝানো bojhano
extra *adj* বেশি beshi, অতিরিক্ত otirikto
extraordinary *adj* অসাধারণ ɔshadharon
extremely *adv* ভীষণ bhishon, অত্যন্ত ɔttonto
eye *n* চোখ cokh

F

fabric *n* কাপড় kapoṛ
face *n* মুখ mu:kh
fact *n* তথ্য tɔttho, সত্য shɔtto
factory *n* কারখানা karkhana
fail *vb* ব্যর্থ হওয়া bærtho hɔowa
faint *adj* দুর্বল durbol
faith *n* আস্থা astha, বিশ্বাস bisshash, ভরসা bhɔrosha
fall *vb* পড়া pɔṛa, পড়ে যাওয়া poṛe jaowa
false *adj* ভুল bhu:l
familiar *adj* চেনা cena, পরিচিত poricito
family *n* পরিবার poribar, সংসার shɔngshar
famous *adj* বিখ্যাত bikkhato
fan *n* পাখা pakha
far *adv* দূরে du:re
farewell *n* বিদায় biday
farm *n* খামার khamar
farmer *n* চাষী cashi, কৃষক krishok
fast *adj, adv* জোরে jore, দ্রুত druto
fat *n* চর্বি corbi; *adj* মোটা moṭa, স্থুল sthulo
fatal *adj* মারাত্মক marattok
father *n* বাবা baba, আব্বা abba, পিতা pita
fault *n* ত্রুটি truṭi, ভুল bhu:l
favor *n* উপকার upokar

fear *n* ভয় bhɔy
feel *vb* টের পাওয়া ṭer paowa, বোধ করা bodh kɔra
feeling *n* অনুভুতি onubhuti
female *adj* স্ত্রীজাতীয় strijatiyo
ferry *n* ফেরি pheri, খেয়া kheya
festival *n* উৎসব utshɔb
fever *n* জ্বর jɔr
few *adj* কয়েক kɔyek
field *n* মাঠ ma:ṭh
fig *n* ডুমুর ḍumur
fight *n* সংগ্রাম shɔnggram, লড়াই lɔṛai; *vb* লড়াই করা lɔṛai kɔra
fill *vb* ভরা bhɔra, ভরানো bhɔrano
film *n* চলচ্চিত্র cɔloccitro, ছবি chobi
final *adj* অন্তিম ontim, শেষ, shesh
find *vb* পাওয়া paowa
fine *adj* চিকন cikon
finger *n* আঙ্গুল anggul
finish *vb* সারা shara, শেষ করা shesh kɔra
fire *n* আগুন agun
firefly *n* জোনাকি jonaki
first *adj, adv* প্রথম prothom
fish *n* মাছ ma:ch
fit *adj* (*suitable*) উপযুক্ত upojukto; (*healthy*) সুস্থ shustho
fix *vb* (*repair*) মেরামত করা meramot kɔra
flat *adj* চেপটা cepṭa; *n* (*apartment*) ফ্ল্যাট phlæṭ
flavor *n* স্বাদ sha:d
flight *n* বিমান যাত্রা biman jatra
flirt *vb* ছিনালি করা chinali kɔra
float *vb* ভাসা bhasha
flood *n* বন্যা bɔnna, বান ba:n
floor *n* মেঝে mejhe
flour *n* ময়দা mɔyda, আটা aṭa
flower *n* ফুল phu:l
flu *n* সর্দিজ্বর shordijjɔr
flute *n* বাঁশি bãshi

fly *vb* ওড়া oṛa; *n* মাছি machi
fog *n* কুয়াশা kuwasha
follow *vb* অনুসরণ করা onushɔron kɔra
food *n* খাবার khabar
fool *n* বোকা boka
foolish *adj* বোকা boka, মূর্খ murkho
foot *n* পা pa:
football *n* ফুটবল phuṭbɔl
for *prep* জন্য jɔnno, জন্যে jɔnne
forbid *vb* নিষেধ করা nishedh kɔra
force *n* জোর jor
foreign *adj* বিদেশি bideshi
foreigner *n* বিদেশি bideshi
forever *adv* চিরদিন cirodin, চিরকাল cirokal
forget *vb* ভোলা bhola, ভুলে যাওয়া bhule jaowa
forgive *vb* ক্ষমা করা khɔma kɔra
fork *n* কাঁটা চামচ kãṭa camoc
fox *n* শিয়াল shiyal
free *adj* স্বাধীন shadhin, মুক্ত mukto
freedom *n* স্বাধনীতা shadhinota, মুক্তি mukti
frequently *adv* প্রায়ই prayi, হামেশা hamesha
fresh *adj* টাটকা ṭaṭka, তাজা taja
friend *n* বন্ধু bondhu
friendly *adj* মিশুক mishuk
friendship *n* বন্ধুত্ব bondhutto
frightening *adj* ভয়ঙ্কর bhɔyonkɔr
frog *n* ব্যাঙ bæng
from *prep* থেকে theke
front *n* সামনা shamna, মুখ mukh
fruit *n* ফল phɔl
fuel *n* জ্বালানি jalani
full *adj* ভরা bhɔra, ভরতি bhorti
fun *n* ফুর্তি phurti, মজা mɔja
function *vb* চলা cɔla, কাজ করা kaj kɔra; *n* (*use*) ব্যবহার bæbohar; (*ceremony*) অনুষ্ঠান onusṭhan
funny *adj* মজাদার mɔjadar, রসিক roshik

fur *n* পশম pɔshom
furniture *n* আসবাব ashbab
futile *adj* ব্যর্থ bærtho
future *n* ভবিষ্যৎ bhobishɔt

G

gain *n* লাভ la:bh
gambling *n* জুয়াখেলা juwakhæla
game *n* খেলনা khælna, খেলা khæla
Ganges *n* গঙ্গা gɔngga
gap *n* ফাঁক phã:k
garbage *n* ময়লা mɔyla
garden *n* বাগান bagan
garlic *n* রসুন roshun
gas *n* গ্যাস gæs
gate *n* গেট geṭ
gay *adj* (*homosexual*) সমকামী shɔmokami; (*happy*) আমুদে amude
gecko *n* টিকটিকি ṭikṭiki
general *adj* সাধারণ shadharon, প্রধান prodhan
gentle *adj* নরম nɔrom, ভদ্র bhɔdro
gentleman *n* ভদ্রলোক bhɔdrolok
genuine *adj* আসল ashol, সত্য sɔtto
get *vb* পাওয়া paowa
get down *vb* নামা nama
get over *vb* (*recover*) ভাল হওয়া bhalo hɔowa
get up *vb* ওঠা oṭha
gift *n* দান da:n, উপহার upohar
girl *n* মেয়ে meye, বালিকা balika
give *vb* দেওয়া deowa
give back *vb* ফেরত দেওয়া pherot deowa
give up *vb* ত্যাগ করা tæg kɔra, ছেড়ে দেওয়া chere deowa
glass *n* (*material*) কাচ ka:c; (*for drinking*) গেলাস gelash
glasses *n* চশমা cɔshma
go *vb* যাওয়া jaowa

goat *n* ছাগল chagol
god *n* দেবতা debota, ভগবান bhɔgoban, ঈশ্বর isshor
gold *n* সোনা shona
good *adj* ভাল bhalo
good-bye *n* খোদা হাফেজ khoda haphej
goodnight *n* শুভরাত্রি shubhoratri
government *n* সরকার shɔrkar
grammar *n* ব্যাকরণ bækoron
granddaughter *n* নাতনি natni
grandfather *n* → *see kinship terms (pages 205-207)*
grandmother *n* → *see kinship terms (pages 205-207)*
grandson *n* নাতি nati
grape *n* আঙুর ফল anggur phɔl
grapefruit *n* জামবুরা jambura
grass *n* ঘাস gha:sh
great *adj* চমৎকার cɔmotkar, দারুণ darun
green *adj* সবুজ shobuj
grocer *n* মুদি mudi
group *n* দল dɔl
grow *vb* বাড়া barạ, বড় হয়ে যাওয়া bɔrọ hoye jaowa
guarantee *n* জামিন jamin
guess *vb* আন্দাজ করা andaj kɔra
guest *n* অতিথি otithi, মেহমান mehoman
guide *vb* (*advise*) উপদেশ দেওয়া upodesh deowa; *n* চালক calok, নেতা neta
guilt *n* দোষ dosh, অপরাধ ɔporadh
gun *n* বন্দুক bonduk
gynecologist *n* স্ত্রীরোগ-চিকিৎসক strirog-cikitshok
gypsy *n* বেদে bede

H

habit *n* অভ্যাস ɔbbhash
hail *n* শিলাবৃষ্টি shilabrishṭi
hair *n* চুল cu:l
hammer *n* হাতুড়ি haturị

hand *n* হাত ha:t
handbag *n* থলি tholi
handkerchief *n* রুমাল rumal
handle *vb* সামলানো shamlano
handle *n* হাতল hatol
handsome *adj* সুন্দর shundor, কমনীয় kɔmoniyo
hang *vb* ঝোলা jhola, ঝোলানো jholano
happen *vb* হওয়া hɔowa, ঘটা ghɔṭa
happiness *n* সুখ shu:kh
happy *adj* খুশি khushi
hard *adj* (*not soft*) শক্ত shɔkto; (*difficult*) কঠিন koṭhin
harm *n* ক্ষতি khoti, হানি hani
harvest *n* ফসল phɔshol
haste *n* তাড়া taṛa
hat *n* টুপি ṭupi
hate *n* ঘৃণা ghrina
have *vb* আছ- ach-, অধিকারে রাখা odhikare rakha
haze *n* কুয়াশা kuwasha
he *pr* সে she:, তিনি tini
head *n* মাথা matha
headache *n* মাথা ধরা matha dhɔra
health *n* স্বাস্থ্য shastho
healthy *adj* সুস্থ shustho, স্বাস্থ্যকর shasthokɔr
hear *vb* শোনা shona
heart *n* মন mon, হৃদয় ridɔy
heat *n* গরম gɔrom, উত্তাপ uttap
heaven *n* স্বর্গ shɔrgo
heavy *adj* ভারী bhaṛi
hell *n* নরক nɔrok
help *n* সাহায্য shahajjo; *vb* সাহায্য করা shahajjo kɔra
helpful *adj* উপকারী upokari
herb *n* উদ্ভিদ udbhid, ওষধি oshodhi
here *adv* এখানে ekhane
hesitate *vb* ইতস্তত করা itostɔto kɔra
hide *vb* লুকানো lukano
high *adj* উচ্চ ucco

hill *n* পাহাড় pahaṛ, পর্বত pɔrbot
Hindi *n* হিন্দি hindi
Hindu *n* হিন্দু hindu
hip *n* পাছা pacha
hire *vb* লাগানো lagano, ভাড়া করা bhaṛa kɔra
historical *adj* ঐতিহাসিক oitihashik
history *n* ইতিহাস itihash
hit *vb* মারা mara, আঘাত করা aghat kɔra
hold *vb* ধরা dhɔra
hole *n* গর্ত gɔrto, ছিদ্র chidro
holiday *n* ছুটি chuṭi
holy *adj* পবিত্র pobitro
home *n* ঘর ghɔr, বাড়ি baṛi
honest *adj* সৎ shɔt, সরল shɔrol
honesty *n* সততা shɔtota
honey *n* মধু modhu
honor *n* মর্যাদা mɔrjada, সম্মান shɔmman
hope *n* আশা asha, কামনা kamona
horizon *n* দিগন্ত digɔnto
horse *n* ঘোড়া ghoṛa
hospital *n* হাসপাতাল hashpatal
hot *adj* (*warm*) গরম gɔrom; (*spicy*) ঝাল jhal, মসলাদার mɔshladar
hotel *n* হোটেল hoṭel
hour *n* ঘণ্টা ghɔnṭa
house *n* ঘর ghɔr, বাসা basha, বাড়ি baṛi
how *adv* কেমন kæmon
huge *adj* প্রকাণ্ড prokanḍo, বিশাল bishal
human *n* মানুষ manush; *adj* মানবিক manobik
humid *adj* আর্দ্র ardro, সেঁতসেঁতে shẽtshẽte
humor *n* হাস্যরস hashorɔsh
hunger *n* ক্ষুধা khudha, খিদা khida
hurry *n* তাড়াহুড়া taṛahuṛa
hurt *n* ব্যথা bætha, বেদনা bedona
hygiene *n* স্বাস্থ্যবিধি shastobidhi

I

I *pr* আমি ami
ice *n* বরফ bɔroph
ice cream *n* আইস ক্রিম ais kri:m
idea *n* ধারণা dharona
identical *adj* একই eki
if *conj* যদি jodi
ill *adj* অসুস্থ ɔshustho
illegal *adj* বেআইনী beaini
illness n অসুখ ɔshukh
immediately *adv* সঙ্গে সঙ্গে shɔngge shɔngge, শিগগিরি shiggiri
impatient *adj* অধীর ɔdhir, অস্থির ɔsthir
important *adj* গুরুত্বপূর্ণ guruttopurno
impossible *adj* অসম্ভব ɔshɔmbhɔb
improve *vb* উন্নতি করা unnoti kɔra
in *prep* ভিতরে bhitore
income *n* আয় ay
inconvenience *n* অসুবিধা ɔshubidha
increase *vb* বাড়া baṛa, বাড়ানো baṛano
indeed *int* তাই তো tai to
independence *n* স্বাধীনতা shadhinota
independent *adj* স্বাধীন shadhin
India *n* ভারত bharot
Indian *adj* ভারতীয় bharotiyo
indigestion *n* বদহজম bɔdhɔjom
industry *n* শ্রমশিল্প sromshilpo
infection *n* সংক্রমণ shɔngkromon
inform *vb* জানানো janano
information *n* খবর khɔbor, জ্ঞাপন gæpon, তথ্য tɔttho
injury *n* ক্ষতি khoti
ink *n* কালি kali
innocent *adj* সরল shɔrol, নির্দোষ nirdosh
insect *n* পোকা poka

inside *prep* ভিতরে bhitore
instead *prep, adv* পরিবর্তে poriborte, বদলে bɔdole
institute *n* প্রতিষ্ঠান protisṭhan
insult *n* অপমান ɔpoman
intelligence *n* বুদ্ধি buddhi
interest *n* আগ্রহ agroho
international *adj* আন্তর্জাতিক antorjatik
interpreter *n* দোভাষী dobhashi, ভাষান্তরিক bhashantorik
interview *n* সাক্ষাৎকার shakkhatkar
intimate *adj* ঘনিষ্ঠ ghonishṭho
introduce *vb* পরিচয় করিয়ে দেওয়া poricɔy koriye deowa
invitation *n* দাওয়াত daowat, নিমন্ত্রণ nimontron
iron *n* (*metal*) লোহা loha; (*appliance*) ইস্ত্রি istri
Islam *n* ইসলাম ধর্ম islam dhɔrmo
Islamic *adj* মুসলিম muslim, মুসলমান musholman
island *n* দ্বীপ di:p
it *pr* তা ta
ivory *n* হস্তিদন্ত hostidɔnto, হাতির দাঁত hatir dãt
ivy *n* লতা lɔta

J

jackal *n* শিয়াল shiyal
jackfruit *n* কাঁঠাল kãṭhal
jail *n* জেল jel, কারাগার karagar
jar *n* বয়াম bɔyam
jasmine *n* জুঁই jũi
jealousy *n* হিংসা hingsha, ঈর্ষা irsha
jewel *n* মণি moni, রত্ন rɔtno
jewelry *n* গয়না gɔyna
job *n* চাকরি cakri
join *vb* সংযুক্ত করা shɔngjukto kɔra
joke *n* তামাশা tamasha, ইয়ারকি iyarki
journal *n* পত্রিকা potrika
journalist *n* সাংবাদিক shangbadik
journey *n* যাত্রা jatra, ভ্রমণ bhrɔmon

joy *n* আনন্দ anondo
judge *vb* বিচার করা bicar kɔra
jug *n* জগ jɔg
juice *n* রস rɔsh
jump *vb* লাফানো laphano, লাফ দেওয়া laph deowa
jungle *n* জঙ্গল jɔnggol
just *adj* (*impartial*) নিরপেক্ষ niropekkho; (*correct*) ঠিক ṭhi:k; *adv* (*only*) মাত্র matro
justice *n* ন্যায় næy, ইনসাফ inshaph *(Muslim)*
jute *n* পাট pa:ṭ

K

kedgeree *n* খিচুড়ি khicuṛi
keep *vb* রাখা rakha
kerosene *n* কেরোসিন keroshin
key *n* চাবি cabi
kick *vb* লাথি মারা laṭhi mara
kidney *n* বৃক্ক brikko, কিডনি kiḍni
kill *vb* মেরে ফেলা mere phæla, হত্যা করা hɔtta kɔra
kind *n* রকম rɔkom, ধরন dhɔron; *adj* দয়ালু dɔyalu
king *n* রাজা raja
kiss *n* চুমু cumu
kitchen *n* রান্না ঘর ranna ghɔr
knee *n* হাঁটু hãṭu
knife *n* ছুরি churi
knock *vb* টোকা দেওয়া ṭoka deowa, ধাক্কা দেওয়া dhakka deowa
knot *n* গিরা gira
know *vb* জানা jana, চেনা cena
knowledge *n* জ্ঞান gæn
Koran *n* কোরান koran

L

lack *n* অভাব ɔbhab
ladder *n* মই moi
lady *n* ভদ্রমহিলা bhɔdromohila, বিবি bibi
lake *n* পুকুর pukur
lamp *n* বাতি bati
land *n* জমি jomi
landlord *n* বাড়িওয়ালা baṛiwala, মালিক malik
language *n* ভাষা bhasha
lantern *n* হারিকেন hariken
large *adj* বড় bɔṛo
last *vb* টিকা ṭika; *adj* (*previous*) গত gɔto; (*final*) শেষ shesh, চরম cɔrom
late *adv* দেরিতে derite
laugh *vb* হাসা hasha
laundry *n* ধোপাখানা dhopakhana
law *n* আইন ain
lawyer *n* উকিল ukil
lay *vb* শোয়ানো showano
layer *n* স্তর stɔr
lazy *adj* অলস ɔlɔsh, কুঁড়ে kũṛe
lead *vb* আগে যাওয়া age jaowa
leader *n* নেতা neta, নায়ক nayok
leaf *n* পাতা pata
learn *vb* শেখা shekha
least *adj, adv* সবচেয়ে কম shɔbceye kɔm; **at least** *adv* অন্তত ɔntoto
leather *n* চামড়া camṛa
leave *vb* চলে যাওয়া cole jaowa
left *adj* (*remaining*) বাকি baki; (*opposite of right*) বাঁ bã:, বাম ba:m
leg *n* পা pa:
legal *adj* বৈধ boidho, আইনত ainoto
leisure *n* অবসর ɔboshor, অবকাশ ɔbokash

lemon *n* লেবু lebu
lend *vb* ধার দেওয়া dhar deowa
lentil *n* ডাল da:l
less *adj, adv* কম kɔm
lesson *n* পাঠ paṭh
let *vb* অনুমতি দেওয়া onumoti deowa
letter *n* চিঠি ciṭhi, পত্র pɔtro
liar *n* মিথ্যুক mitthuk, মিথ্যাবাদী mitthabadi
library *n* গ্রন্থাগার gronthagar, লাইব্রেরি laibreri
lie *vb* (*make false statement*) মিথ্যা কথা বলা mittha kɔtha bɔla; (*lie down*) শোয়া showa; *n* (*false statement*) মিথ্যা কথা mittha kɔtha
life *n* জীবন jibon, প্রাণ pra:n
lift *vb* তোলা tola
light *n* আলো alo; *adj* হালকা halka
lightning *n* বিজলি bijoli
like *prep* মত mɔto; *vb* ভাল লাগা bhalo laga
likely *adv* সম্ভবত shɔmbhɔbɔto
lime *n* (*fruit*) লেবু lebu; (*mineral*) চুন cun
limit *n* সীমা shima
line *n* রেখা rekha
lion *n* সিংহ shingho
lip *n* ঠোঁট ṭhõṭ
literature *n* সাহিত্য shahitto
little *adj* ছোট choto
live *vb* থাকা thaka, বাস করা bash kɔra
living room *n* বসার ঘর bɔshar ghɔr
lizard *n* টিকটিকি ṭikṭiki
loan *n* ঋণ ri:n, দেনা dena, ধার dhar
local *adj* স্থানীয় sthaniyo, আঞ্চলিক ancolik
lock *n* তালা tala
logic *n* যুক্তি jukti
lonely *adj* (*feeling alone*) একা একা æka æka, নিঃসঙ্গ nishɔnggo; (*secluded*) নিরিবিলি niribili
long *adj* লম্বা lɔmba, দীর্ঘ dirgho
look *vb* তাকানো takano, দেখা dækha

look after *vb* দেখাশোনা করা dækhashona kɔra
look back *vb* ফিরে তাকানো phire takano
look down on *vb* ছোট মনে করা choṭo mone kɔra
look for *vb* খোঁজা khõja
lose *vb* হারা hara, হারানো harano
lot, lots *adj* প্রচুর procur
lotus *n* জলপদ্ম jɔlpɔdmo
loud *adj* জোরে jore
love *vb* ভালবাসা bhalobasha; *n* ভালবাসা bhalobasha, প্রেম prem
loyal *adj* বিশ্বস্ত bishosto, আস্থাবান asthaban
luck *n* ভাগ্য bhaggo, কপাল kɔpal
lucky *adj* ভাগ্যবান bhaggoban
luggage *n* মালপত্র malpɔtro
lunch *n* দুপুরের খাবার dupurer khabar
lung *n* ফুসফুস phushphush
lungi *n* (*long loincloth*) লুঙ্গি lungi
luxury *n* বিলাস bilash

M

machine *n* কল kɔl
mad *adj* পাগল pagol
magazine *n* পত্রিকা potrika
magic *n* জাদু jadu
magician *n* জাদুকর jadukɔr
magnet *n* চুম্বক cumbok
maid *n* ঝি jhi:
mail *n* ডাক ḍa:k
main *adj* প্রধান prodhan
majority *n* অধিকাংশ odhikangsho
make *vb* (*do*) করা kɔra; (*prepare*) বানানো banano; (*create*) সৃষ্টি করা srishti kɔra
man *n* (*human being*) মানুষ manush, (*male person*) পুরুষ purush
manager *n* পরিচালক poricalok, শাসক shashok

manner *n* রীতিনীতি ritiniti
many *adj* অনেক ɔnek, বহু bohu
map *n* মানচিত্র mancitro
market *n* হাট ha:ṭ, বাজার bajar
marriage *n* বিয়ে biye, বিবাহ bibaho
marry *vb* বিয়ে করা biye kɔra
massage *n* মালিশ malish
mat *n* মাদুর madur, পাটি paṭi
match *n* দেশলাই desholai, ম্যাচ mæc
matter *n* ব্যাপার bæpar
mattress *n* তোশক toshok
maybe *adv* হয়তো, বোধ হয় hɔyto, bodh hɔy
meal *n* খাবার khabar, আহার ahar
meaning *n* অর্থ ɔrtho, মানে mane
meat *n* মাংস mangsho
mechanic *n* মিস্ত্রি mistri
medical *adj* চিকিৎসামূলক cikitshamulok
medicine *n* (*science*) চিকিৎসাবিদ্যা cikitshabidda; (*treatment*) ওষুধ oshudh
meet *vb* দেখা করা dækha kɔra
meeting *n* সভা shɔbha, অধিবেশন odhibeshon
melon *n* তরমুজ tormuj
melt *vb* গলা gɔla, গলানো gɔlano
memory *n* স্মৃতি sriti
merit *n* গুণ gun
message *n* সংবাদ shɔngbad, খবর khɔbor
metal *n* ধাতু dhatu
method *n* কায়দা kayda, পদ্ধতি pɔddhoti
midday *n* দুপুর dupur
middle *n* মধ্য moddho
midwife *n* দাই dai, ধাইমা dhaima
migraine *n* কঠিন মাথা ধরা koṭhin matha dhɔra
mild *adj* হালকা halka
military *adj* সৈনিক shoinik; *n* সৈন্যদল shoinodɔl
milk *n* দুধ dudh
mind *vb* মনে করা mone kɔra; *n* মন mon

minister *n* মন্ত্রী montri
minute *n* মিনিট miniṭ
mirror *n* আয়না ayna
misfortune *n* দুর্ভাগ্য durbhaggo
miss *vb* বাদ দেওয়া bad deowa
mistake *n* ভুল bhul
misunderstanding *n* ভুল বোঝা bhul bojha
modern *adj* আধুনিক adhunik
modest *adj* নম্র nɔmro, বিনয়ী binoyi
moment *n* মুহূর্ত muhurto
money *n* টাকা ṭaka
mongoose *n* বেজি beji
monk *n* সন্ন্যাসী shɔnnashi
monkey *n* বানর banor
month *n* মাস mash
mood *n* মেজাজ mejaj
moon *n* চাঁদ cãd
more *adj* আরও aro
morning *n* সকাল shɔkal
mosque *n* মসজিদ moshjid
mosquito *n* মশা mɔsha
mosquito net *n* মশারি mɔshari
most *adj* অধিকাংশ odhikangsho
mother *n* মা ma, আম্মা amma
mountain *n* পাহাড় pahaṛ, পর্বত pɔrbot
mouse *n* ইঁদুর ĩdur
mouth *n* মুখ mukh
move *vb* চলা cɔla
movie *n* চলচ্চিত্র cɔloccitro
much *adj* অনেক ɔnek
mud *n* কাদা kada
mug *n* মগ mɔg
murder *n* খুন khun
muscle *n* পেশী peshi
museum *n* জাদুঘড় jadughɔr
mushroom *n* ছাতা chata

music *n* সঙ্গীত shonggit
musician *n* সঙ্গীতকার shonggitokar
Muslim *n* মুসলমান musholman; *adj* মুসলিম muslim
mustard *n* সরিষা shorisha
mustard oil *n* সরিষার তেল shorishar tel

N

nail *n* পেরেক perek
naked *adj* নেংটা nengṭa, উলঙ্গ ulɔngo
name *n* নাম nam
namely *adv* যেমন jæmon, অর্থাৎ ɔrthat
narrow *adj* সরু shoru
nasty *adj* বিছরি bichri, নোংরা nongra
nation *n* জাতি jati
national *adj* জাতীয় jatiyo
nationality *n* জাতিত্ব jatitto
natural *adj* (*of nature*) প্রাকৃতিক prakritik; (*normal*) স্বাভাবিক shabhabik
naturally *adv* অবশ্যই ɔboshoi
nature *n* (*natural life*) প্রকৃতি prokriti; (*characteristic*) *n* স্বভাব shɔbhab
nausea *n* বমি bomi
near *adv, prep* কাছে kache
nearly *adv* প্রায় pray
necessary *adj* প্রয়োজনীয় proyojoniyo
neck *n* ঘাড় ghaṛ
necklace *n* মালা mala
need *n* দরকার dɔrkar, চাহিদা cahida,
needle *n* সুই shui
needless *adj* অপ্রয়োজনীয় ɔproyojoniyo
neglect *vb* অবহেলা করা ɔbohæla kɔra
neighbor *n* প্রতিবেশী protibeshi
nerve *n* স্নায়ু snayu
net *n* (*fishing net*) জাল jal; (*mosquito net*) মশারি mɔshari
never *adv* কখনও ... না kɔkhono ... na

new *adj* নতুন notun
news *n* খবর khɔbor, সংবাদ shɔngbad
newspaper *n* খবরের কাগজ khɔborer kagoj
New Year *n* নববর্ষ nɔbobɔrsho
next *adj* আগামী agami
nice *adj* মনোরম monorom
night *n* রাত rat
no *adv* না na
nobody *pr* কেউ ... না keu ... na
noise *n* শব্দ shɔbdo, আওয়াজ aowaj, হইচই hoicoi
none *n* (*nothing*) কিছু ... না kichu ... na; (*no one*) কেউ ... না keu ... na
nonsense *n* আজেবাজে ajebaje, আবোলতাবোল aboltabol
noon *n* দুপুর dupur
normal *adj* স্বাভাবিক shabhabik
north *n* উত্তর uttor
nose *n* নাক nak
not *adv* না na; **not at all** *adv* মোটেই ...না moṭei ... na
notebook *n* খাতা khata
nothing *pr* কিছু ... না kichu ... na
notice *vb* টের পাওয়া ṭer paowa
novel *n* উপন্যাস uponnash
now *adv* এখন ækhon
nowadays *adv* আজকাল ajkal
nowhere *adv* কোথাও ... না kothao ... na
number *n* সংখ্যা shɔngkkha
nurse *n* নার্স nars, সেবক shebok (*m*), সেবিকা shebika (*f*)
nursing *n* সেবা sheba
nut *n* বাদাম badam
nutmeg *n* জায়ফল jayphɔl
nutrition *n* পুষ্টি pushṭi

O

object *n* বস্তু bostu, জিনিস jinish
objection *n* আপত্তি apotti

obvious *adj* সুস্পষ্ট shuspɔshṭo
occasionally *adv* সময় সময় shɔmɔy shɔmɔy
occupation *n* পেশা pesha
ocean *n* সাগর shagor, সমুদ্র shomudro
odd *adj* অদ্ভুত ɔdbhut
odor *n* গন্ধ gɔndho
of course *adv* নিশ্চয় nishcɔy, অবশ্য ɔbossho
offensive *adj* বিরক্তিকর biroktikor
offer *n* প্রস্তাব prostab
office *n* আপিস apis, দপ্তর dɔptor
often *adv* প্রায়ই prayi
oil *n* তেল tel
ointment *n* মলম mɔlom
OK *adv* ঠিক আছে ṭhik ache
old *adj* (*of things*) পুরানো purano; (*of people*) বুড়ো buṛo, বুড়া buṛa (*m*), বুড়ি buṛi (*f*)
olive *n* জলপাই jɔlpai
omit *vb* বাদ দেওয়া bad deowa
on *prep* (*above*) উপর upor
once *adv* একবার ækbar
oneself *pr* নিজ ni:j, আপন apon
onion *n* পিঁয়াজ pĩyaj, পেঁয়াজ pẽyaj
only *adj* একমাত্র ekmatro; *adv* শুধু shudhu, কেবল kebol, মাত্র matro
open *vb, adj* খোলা khola
opinion *n* মত mɔt
opportunity *n* সুযোগ shujog
opposite *adj* বিপরীত biporit
or *conj* বা ba, অথবা ɔthoba
orange *n, adj* কমলা kɔmla
order *n* হুকুম hukum, আদেশ adesh
ordinary *adj* সাধারণ shadharon, স্বাভাবিক shabhabik
organization *n* সংস্থা shɔngstha
origin *n* উৎপত্তি utpotti
original *adj* আদিম adim, মৌলিক moulik
other *adj* অন্য ɔnno

otherwise *conj* না হলে na hole
ought *vb* উচিত ucit
out *adv, prep* বাইরে baire
outside *adv, prep* বাইরে baire
oven *n* চুলা cula
over *adv* উপরে upore, অতি- oti
own *adj* নিজের nijer, আপন apon
owner *n* অধিকারী odhikari, মালিক malik
ox *n* ষাঁড় shãṛ
oxygen *n* অম্লজান ɔmlojan

P

paddy *n* ধান dhan
padlock *n* তালা tala
page *n* পাতা pata
pain *n* ব্যথা bætha, বেদনা, bedona
paint *n* রং rɔng; *vb* (*do artwork*) আঁকা ãka; (*add color*) রঙ দেওয়া rɔng deowa
pan *n* কড়াই kɔṛai
pants *n* প্যান্ট pænṭ
papaya *n* পেঁপে pẽpe
paper *n* কাগজ kagoj
park *n* পার্ক park
parliament *n* সংসদ shɔngshɔd
parrot *n* টিয়া-পাখি ṭiya-pakhi
part *n* অংশ ɔngsho, ভাগ bhag
particular *adj* বিশেষ bishesh
partner *n* সঙ্গী shonggi; (*shareholder*) অংশীদার ongshidar
party *n* (*group*) দল, dɔl; (*get-together*) পার্টি parṭi
pass *vb* (*spend time*) কাটানো kaṭano; (*go past*) পার হওয়া par hɔowa
passenger *n* যাত্রী jatri
passion *n* ভাবাবেগ bhababeg
passport *n* পাসপোর্ট pasporṭ
past *n* অতীত otit

path *n* পথ pɔth
patience *n* ধৈর্য dhoirjo
patient *n* রোগী rogi
pay *vb* টাকা দেওয়া ṭaka deowa
peace *n* শান্তি shanti
peaceful *adj* শান্ত shanto
peacock *n* ময়ুর moyur
peanut *n* বাদাম badam
pen *n* কলম kɔlom
penalty *n* শাস্তি shasti
pencil *n* পেনসিল pensil
people *n* লোকজন lokjɔn
pepper *n* গোল মরিচ gol moric
perfect *adj* নিখুঁত nikhũt
perhaps *adv* হয়তো hɔyto, বোধ হয় bodh hɔy
permission *n* অনুমতি onumoti
person *n* ব্যক্তি bekti, লোক lok
personal *n* ব্যক্তিগত bektigɔto
petrol *n* তেল tel, পেট্রল peṭrol
pharmacy *n* ওষুধের দোকান oshudher dokan
philosophy *n* দর্শনশাস্ত্র dɔrshonshastro
phone *n* টেলিফোন ṭeliphon
photo *n* তোলা ছবি tola chobi, ফোটো phoṭo
photography *n* আলোকচিত্র alokcitro
physical *adj* (*natural*) প্রাকৃতিক prakritik; (*of the body*) শারীরিক sharirik, দৈহিক doihik
picture *n* ছবি, চিত্র chobi, citro
piece *n* টুকরা ṭukra
pig *n* শূকর shukor
pigeon *n* কবুতর kobutor
pill *n* বড়ি boṛi
pillow *n* বালিশ balish
pineapple *n* আনারস anarɔsh
pink *adj* গোলাপী golapi
pipe *n* নল nɔl
place *n* জায়গা jayga, স্থান sthan

plain *adj* সমতল shɔmotɔl
plan *n* পরিকল্পনা porikɔlpona
plane *n* বিমান biman
planet *n* গ্রহ groho
plant *n* চারাগাছ caragach; *vb* লাগানো lagano
plate *n* থালা thala
play *vb* খেলা khæla; *n* নাটক naṭok
playing cards *n* তাস tash
please *int* দয়া করে dɔya kore
pleasure *n* আনন্দ anondo
plenty *adj* বহু bohu
pocket *n* পকেট pɔkeṭ
poem *n* কবিতা kobita
poet *n* কবি kobi
poetry *n* কাব্য kabbo
poison *n* বিষ bish
police *n* পুলিশ pulish
police station *n* থানা thana
politics *n* রাজনীতি rajniti
pollution *n* দূষণ dushon
pomegranate *n* ডালিম ḍalim
pond *n* পুকুর pukur
poor *adj* গরিব gorib
popular *adj* জনপ্রিয় jɔnopriyo
population *n* জনসংখ্যা jɔnoshɔngkha
pork *n* শূকরের মাংস shukorer mangsho
port *n* বন্দর bɔndor
possible *adj* সম্ভব shɔmbhɔb
post office *n* ডাকঘর ḍakghɔr
pot *n* ডেকচি, হাঁড়ি ḍekci, hãri
potato *n* আলু alu
powder *n* চূর্ণ curno, গুঁড়া gũṛa
power *n* (*ability*) ক্ষমতা khɔmota; (*strength*) শক্তি shokti
practice *n* রীতি riti, চর্চা cɔrca
praise *n* প্রশংসা proshɔngsha
prayer *n* (*religious intercession*) প্রার্থনা prarthona;

(*request*) আর্জি arji, অনুরোধ onurodh; (*Muslim prayer*) নামাজ namaj
precious *adj* মূল্যবান mulloban
pregnant *adj* গর্ভবতী gɔrbhoboti
prepare *vb* প্রস্তুত করা prostut kɔra, তৈরি করা toiri kɔra
present *n* উপহার upohar
president *n* রাষ্ট্রপতি rasṭropoti, সভাপতি shɔbhapoti
pressure *n* চাপ ca:p
pretend *vb* ভান করা bha:n kɔra
pretty *adj* সুন্দর shundor, শোভন shobhon
price *n* দাম dam
pride *n* গর্ব gɔrbo
priest *n* (*Hindu*) যাজক jajok, পুরোহিত purohit; (*Muslim*) মোল্লা molla, ইমাম imam; (*Christian*) পাদরি padri
print *vb* ছাপা chapa, ছাপানো chapano
prison *n* জেল jel, কারাগার karagar
private *adj* ব্যক্তিগত bektigɔto
probably *adv* সম্ভবত shɔmbhɔbɔto
problem *n* সমস্যা shɔmossha
profession *n* পেশা pesha
profit *n* লাভ la:bh
progress *n* অগ্রগতি ɔgrogoti, উন্নতি unnoti
project *n* প্রকল্প prokɔlpo
promise *vb* কথা দেওয়া kɔtha deowa
protect *vb* রক্ষা করা rɔkkha kɔra
proud *adj* গর্বিত gorbito
province *n* প্রদেশ prodesh
public *n* জনসাধারণ jɔnoshadharon
pull *vb* টানা ṭana
pullover *n* গরম গেঞ্জি gɔrom genji, সুয়েটার suweṭar
pure *adj* খাঁটি khãṭi, শুচি shuci
purpose *n* উদ্দেশ্য uddessho
push *vb* ঠেলা ṭhæla
put *vb* রাখা rakha, থওয়া thɔowa
put down *vb* বসানো bɔshano
put off *vb* মুলতবি রাখা multobi rakha

put on *vb* পরা pɔra
put out *vb* নিবানো nibano
put up with *vb* সহ্য করা shɔjjo kɔra
puzzle *n* ধাঁধা dhãdha

Q

quarrel *n* ঝগড়া jhɔgṛa
quarry *n* খনি khoni
queen *n* রানী rani
question *n* প্রশ্ন proshno, জিজ্ঞাসা jiggasha
queue *n* সিরিয়াল siriyal
quick *adj* দ্রুত druto
quiet *adj* (*silent*) চুপচুপ cupcap, নীরব nirob; (*peaceful*) শান্ত shanto
quit *vb* ছেড়ে যাওয়া cheṛe jaowa
quite *adv* বেশ besh

R

rabbit *n* খরগোশ khɔrgosh
race *n* (*people*) জাতি jati; (*competition*) প্রতিযোগিতা protijogita
radiator *n* শীতাতপ-নিয়ন্ত্রণ shitatop-niyontron
radical *adj* মৌলিক moulik
radio *n* বেতার, রেডিও reḍio
radish *n* মূলা mula
railroad, railway *n* রেলপথ relpɔth
rain *n* বৃষ্টি brishṭi, বর্ষা bɔrsha
raise *vb* তোলা tola
raisin *n* কিশমিশ kismis
Ramadan *n* রোজা roja
rat *n* ইঁদুর ĩdur, ইন্দুর indur
rather *adv* বরং bɔrong
rational *adj* যুক্তিবাদী juktibad

raw *adj* কাঁচা kãca
razor *n* ক্ষুর khur
reach *vb* নাগাল পাওয়া nagal paowa
read *vb* পড়া pɔṛa
ready *adj* প্রস্তুত prostut, তৈরি toiri
real *adj* আসল ashol, বাস্তব bastob
reason *n* কারণ karon
receive *vb* পাওয়া paowa
recently *adv* সম্প্রতি shɔmproti, ইদানীং idaning
recognize *vb* চেনা cena
recommend *vb* সুপারিশ করা shuparish kɔra
red *adj* লাল lal
reduce *vb* কমানো kɔmano
refrigerator *n* হিমায়নযন্ত্র himayonjɔntro, ফ্রিজ phrij
regard *vb* বিবেচনা করা bibecona kɔra
region *n* এলাকা elaka, অঞ্চল ɔncɔl
regret *n* দুঃখ dukkho
regular *adj* নিয়মিত niyomito
reject *vb* ফেলে দেওয়া phele deowa, অস্বীকার করা ɔshikar kɔra
relationship *n* সম্পর্ক shɔmpɔrko
relative *n* আত্মীয় attiyo
religion *n* ধর্ম dhɔrmo
rely on *vb* নির্ভর করা nirbhor kɔra
remain *vb* থাকা thaka
remember *vb* মনে রাখা mɔne rakha
remove *vb* সরানো shɔrano
rent *n* খাজনা khajna, ভাড়া bhaṛa
repair *vb* মেরামত করা meramot kɔra
reply *vb* জবাব দেওয়া jɔbab deowa
reporter *n* সাংবাদিক shangbadik
request *n* অনুরোধ onurodh
reserve *vb* আগে বুক করা age buk kɔra
residence *n* বাসভবন bashbhɔbon
rest *n* (*relaxation*) বিশ্রাম bisram; (*remainder*) বাকি baki
restaurant *n* রেস্তোরাঁ restorã

result *n* ফল phɔl
return *vb* ফেরা phera, ফিরে আসা phire asha, ফিরে যাওয়া phire jaowa
rheumatism *n* বাত bat
rhythm *n* ছন্দ chɔndo, তাল tal
rice *n* (*in paddy*) ধান dhan; (*uncooked*) চাল cal, চাউল caul; (*cooked*) ভাত bhat
rich *adj* ধনী dhoni
rickshaw *n* রিকশা riksha
right *n* অধিকার odhikar; *adj* (*correct*) ঠিক ṭhik, সঠিক shɔṭhik; (*opposite of left*) ডান ḍan, ডাইন ḍain
ring *n* আঙটি angṭi
ripe *adj* পাকা paka
rise *vb* ওঠা oṭha
risk *n* ঝুঁকি jhũki
river *n* নদী nodi
riverbank *n* তীর tir
road *n* রাস্তা rasta, পথ pɔth
rock *n* পাথর pathor
role *n* ভূমিকা bhumika
roof *n* ছাদ chad
room *n* ঘর ghɔr
root *n* শিকড় shikoṛ, মূল mu:l
rope *n* দড়ি doṛi
rose *n* গোলাপ golap
rotten *adj* পচা pɔca
round *adj* গোল gol
routine *n* নিয়ম niyom
row *n* সারি shari
rude *adj* অসভ্য ɔshɔbbho, অভদ্র ɔbhɔdro
rule *n* শাসন shashon
rumor *n* গুজব gujob, গল্পগুজব gɔlpogujob
run *vb* দৌড়ানো douṛano, ছোটা choṭa

S

sack *n* বস্তা bɔsta
sacred *adj* পবিত্র pobitro
sad *adj* মন খারাপ mon kharap, বিষণ্ণ bishɔnno
sadness *n* দুঃখ dukho, বিষণ্ণতা bishɔnnota
safe *adj* নিরাপদ nirapod
safety *n* নিরাপত্তা nirapotta
salary *n* বেতন beton
salt *n* লবণ lɔbon, নুন nun
same *adj* একই eki
sand *n* বালু balu, বালি bali
sandal *n* চটি coṭi, স্যান্ডাল sænḍal
sane *adj* সুস্থ মনের shustho mɔner
saree *n* শাড়ি shaṛi
sauce *n* ঝোল jhol
save *vb* বাঁচানো bãcano
say *vb* বলা bɔla
scarf *n* ওড়না oṛna
scenery *n* দৃশ্য drissho
school *n* স্কুল skul, বিদ্যালয় biddalɔy
science *n* বিজ্ঞান biggæn
scissors *n* কাঁচি kãci, কেচি keci
scorpion *n* বিছা bicha
scream *vb* চিৎকার করা citkar kɔra
script *n* লিপি lipi
sea *n* সাগর shagor, সমুদ্র shomudro
season *n* ঋতু ritu, কাল kal
seat *n* চেয়ার ceyar, সিট si:ṭ, বসার জায়গা bɔshar jayga
see *vb* দেখা dækha
seed *n* বিচি bici, বীজ bi:j
seem *vb* মনে হওয়া mɔne hɔowa
seldom *adv* কম kɔm
select *vb* বেছে নেওয়া beche neowa, পছন্দ করা pɔchondo kɔra
self *n* নিজ nij, নিজে nije

selfish *adj* স্বার্থপর sharthopɔr
sell *vb* বেচা bæca, বিক্রি করা bikri kɔra
send *vb* পাঠানো paṭhano
sense *n* (*meaning*) অর্থ ɔrtho, মানে mane; (*ability to perceive*) বোধ bodh
sensible *adj* সুবুদ্ধিপূর্ণ shubuddhipurno
sentence *n* (*part of speech*) বাক্য bakko; (*punishment*) শাস্তি shasti
separate *adj* আলাদা alada, বিছিন্ন bichinno
serious *adj* (*solemn*) গম্ভীর gombhir; (*important*) গুরুত্বপূর্ণ guruttopurno
service *n* সেবা sheba
set off *vb* রওনা হওয়া rɔona hɔowa
several *adj* কয়েক kɔyek
severe *adj* কড়া kɔṛa, কঠোর kɔṭhor
sew *vb* সেলাই করা shelai kɔra
sex *n* লিঙ্গ linggo
shade *n* ছায়া chaya
shadow *n* ছায়া chaya
shady *adj* ছায়াময় chayamɔy
shake *vb* ঝাঁকা jhãka
shame *n* লজ্জা lɔjja, শরম shɔrom
shampoo *n* শ্যাম্পু shæmpu
shape *n* রূপ ru:p, আকার akar
share *n* অংশ ɔngsho, ভাগ bhag; *vb* ভাগ করা bhag kɔra, অংশ নেওয়া ɔngsho neowa
sharp *adj* ধারালো dharalo
sheep *n* ভেড়া bhæṛa
sheet *n* চাদর cador
shelf *n* তাক tak
shelter *n* আশ্রয় asrɔy
ship *n* জাহাজ jahaj
shirt *n* জামা jama, সার্ট sharṭ
shiver *vb* কাঁপা kãpa
shock *n* আঘাত aghat, দাগা daga
shoe *n* জুতা juta, জুতো juto

shop *n* দোকান dokan
short *adj* খাটো khaṭo
shortage *n* অভাব ɔbhab
shorts *n* হাফ-প্যান্ট ha:ph-pænṭ
shoulder *n* কাঁধ kãdh
shout *vb* চেঁচানো cẽcano, চিৎকার করা citkar kɔra
show *vb* দেখানো dekhano
shrimp *n* চিংড়ি মাছ cingṛi mach
shrine *n* তীর্থস্থান tirthosthan
shut *adj* বন্ধ bɔndho
sick *adj* অসুস্থ ɔshustho
sickness *n* অসুখ ɔshukh
side *n* পাশ pash
sight *n* দৃষ্টি drishṭi
sign *n* চিহ্ন cinho
signature *n* সই shoi
silence *n* নীরবতা nirɔbota
silent *adj* নীরব nirɔb, চুপচাপ cupcap
silk *n* রেশম reshom
silly *adj* দুষ্টু dushṭu, পাজি paji
silver *n* রূপা rupa
similar *adj* প্রায় একই pray eki
simple *adj* সরল shɔrol, সহজ shɔhoj
sin *n* পাপ pap
since *prep* থেকে theke
sing *vb* গাওয়া gaowa
singer *n* গায়ক gayok (*m*), গায়িকা gayika (*f*)
sister *n* বোন bon
sit *vb* বসা bɔsha
situation *n* অবস্থা ɔbostha
skin *n* চামড়া camṛa
sleep *vb* ঘুমানো ghumano; *n* ঘুম ghum
slow *adj* ধীরে dhire
slowly *adv* আস্তে আস্তে aste aste
slum *n* বস্তি bosti
small *adj* ছোট choṭo

smell *n* গন্ধ gɔndho, ঘ্রাণ ghran
smile *vb* হাসা hasha; *n* হাসি hashi
smoke *n* ধুম dhum, ধোঁয়া dhõwa
snake *n* সাপ shap
snow *n* তুষার tushar
so *adv* তাই tai
so much *adv* এতো eto
soap *n* সাবান shaban
social *adj* সামাজিক shamajik
society *n* সমাজ shɔmaj
sock *n* মোজা moja
soft *adj* নরম nɔrom
soil *n* মাটি maṭi
soldier *n* সৈনিক shoinik, সেনা shena
solitude *n* নির্জনতা nirjɔnota
solution *n* সমাধান shɔmadhan
some *adj* কিছু kichu
somebody *n* কেউ keu
someone *n* কেউ keu
something *n* কিছু kichu
sometimes *adv* সময় সময় shɔmɔy shɔmɔy
son *n* ছেলে chele, পুত্র putro, সন্তান shɔntan
song *n* গান gan
soon *adv* একটু পরে ekṭu pɔre, শিগগির shiggir
sorry *adj* দুঃখিত dukhito
sort *n* রকম rɔkom, প্রকার prokar
soul *n* আত্মা atma
sound *n* শব্দ shɔbdo, আওয়াজ aowaj
soup *n* সুপ sup
sour *adj* টক ṭɔk
south *n* দক্ষিণ dokkhin
space *n* জায়গা jayga, স্থান sthan
speak *vb* (*utter*) বলা bɔla; (*converse*) কথা বলা kɔtha bɔla
special *adj* বিশেষ bishesh
specialist *n* বিশেষজ্ঞ bisheshoggo
spelling *n* বানান banan

spend *vb* (*money*) খরচ করা khɔroc kɔra, (*time*) কাটানো kaṭano
spice *n* মসলা mɔshla
spicy *adj* ঝাল jhal
spider *n* মাকড়সা makoṛsha
spinach *n* পালং শাক palong sha:k
spite, in spite of *conj* সত্ত্বেও shɔtteo
spoil *vb* নষ্ট করা nɔshṭo kɔra
spoon *n* চামচ camoc
sport *n* খেলাধূলা khæladhula
spread *vb* পাতা pata
spring *n* (*season*) বসন্তকাল bɔshontokal; (*source of water*) ঝরনা jhɔrna
spy *n* গুপ্তচর guptocor
squirrel *n* কাঠবিড়ালি kaṭhbiṛali
stage *n* মঞ্চ mɔnco
stairs *n* সিঁড়ি shĩṛi
stale *adj* বাসি bashi
stamp *n* টিকিট ṭikiṭ
stand *vb* দাঁড়ানো dãṛano
star *n* তারা tara
start *n* আরম্ভ arombho, শুরু shuru
state *n* (*condition*) অবস্থা ɔbostha; (*nation*) রাজ্য rajjo
station *n* ইষ্টেশন isṭeshon
stay *vb* থাকা thaka, রওয়া rɔowa
steal *vb* চুরি করা curi kɔra
stick *n* লাঠি laṭhi
stiff *adj* শক্ত shɔkto
still *adj* নীরব nirob, শান্ত shanto; *adv* এখনও ækhono
stir *vb* নড়া nɔṛa, নাড়া naṛa
stomach *n* পেট peṭ
stone *n* পাথর pathor
stop *vb* থামা thama, থামানো thamano
storm *n* ঝড় jhɔṛ, তুফান tuphan
story *n* গল্প gɔlpo, কাহিনী kahini
stove *n* চুলা cula

straight *adj* (*ahead*) সোজা shɔja; (*direct*) সরাসরি shɔrashori
strange *adj* (*unknown*) অচেনা ɔcena; (*weird*) অদ্ভুত ɔdbhut
stranger *n* অচেনা লোক ɔcena lok
street *n* রাস্তা rasta
strike *n* হরতাল hɔrtal
string *n* দড়ি doṛi
strong *adj* শক্তিশালী shoktishali, প্রবল probɔl
stubborn *adj* জেদী jedi
student *n* ছাত্র chatro (*m*), ছাত্রী chatri (*f*)
stupid *adj* বোকা boka, মূর্খ murkho
subway *n* পাতাল রেল patal rel
succeed *vb* সফল হওয়া shɔphɔl hɔowa
such *adj* এমন æmon
suck *vb* চুষা cusha
sudden *adj* হঠাৎ hɔṭhat
suffer *vb* কষ্ট পাওয়া kɔshṭo paowa, ভোগ করা bhog kɔra
sufficient *adj* যথেষ্ট jɔtheshṭo
sugar *n* চিনি cini
sugarcane *n* আখ akh
suit *vb* মানানো manano; *n* সুট suṭ
suitable *adj* উপযুক্ত upojukto, যোগ্য joggo
suitcase *n* সুটকেস suṭkes
summer *n* গরমকাল gɔromkal, গ্রীষ্মকাল grisshokal
sun *n* সূর্য shurjo, রোদ rod
sunrise *n* সূর্যোদয় shurjodɔy
sunset *n* সূর্যাস্ত shurjasto
sunshine *n* রোদ rod
support *n* সমর্থন shɔmorthon
sure *adj* নিশ্চিত nishcito
surely *adv* অবশ্য ɔbossho
surname *n* পদবি pɔdobi
surprise *n* আশ্চর্য ashcorjo, বিস্ময় bisshɔy
survive *vb* বাঁচা bãca, বেঁচে থাকা bẽce thaka
suspect *vb* সন্দেহ করা shɔndeho kɔra

swallow *vb* গিলা gila
swear *vb* শপথ করা shɔpɔth kɔra
sweat *n* ঘাম gha:m
sweet *adj* মিষ্টি mishṭi
swim *vb* সাঁতার কাটা shãtar kaṭa

T

table *n* টেবিল ṭebil
tablet *n* বড়ি boṛi
tact *n* সুবিচার shubicar
tail *n* লেজ lej
tailor *n* দরজি dorji
take *vb* নেওয়া neowa
take away *vb* সরিয়ে নিয়ে যাওয়া shoriye niye jaowa
take off *vb* খোলা khola
take over *vb* নিয়ন্ত্রণ করা niyontron kɔra
talk *vb* কথা বলা kɔtha bɔla
tall *adj* লম্বা lɔmba
tamarind *n* তেঁতুল tẽtul
tax *n* কর kɔr, খাজনা khajna
taxi *n* ট্যাকসি ṭæksi
tea *n* চা ca
teach *vb* শেখানো shekhano
teacher *n* (*in a school*) শিক্ষক shikkhok (*m*), শিক্ষিকা shikkhika (*f*); (*spiritual guide*) গুরু guru
tear *n* চোখের জল cokher jɔl, কান্না kanna; *vb* ছেঁড়া chẽṛa, ছিন্ন করা chinno kɔra
telephone *n* টেলিফোন ṭeliphon
television *n* টেলিভিশন ṭelibhishon
tell *vb* বলা bɔla, জানানো janano
temperature *n* তাপ tap
temple *n* মন্দির mondir
tent *n* তাঁবু tãbu
terrorism *n* সন্ত্রাসবাদ shɔntrashbad
terrorist *n* সন্ত্রাসী shɔntrashi

test *n* পরীক্ষা porikkha
than *conj* চেয়ে ceye
thank *vb* ধন্যবাদ দেওয়া dhɔnnobad deowa
thanks *int* ধন্যবাদ dhɔnnobad
that *pr* তা ta; *conj* যে je
then *adv, conj* তখন tɔkhon, সে সময় she shɔmɔy
there *adv* সেখানে shekhane
therefore *conj* তাই tai, অতএব ɔtoeb, সুতরাং shutorang
thick *adj* মোটা moṭa, ঘন ghɔno
thief *n* চোর cor
thin *adj* পাতলা patla, রোগা roga
thing *n* জিনিস jinish, বস্তু bostu
think *vb* ভাবা bhaba, মনে করা mɔne kɔra
thought *n* চিন্তা cinta, ভাবনা bhabna
throat *n* গলা gɔla
throw *vb* ছুড়ে ফেলা chuṛe phæla
throw away *vb* ফেলে দেওয়া phele deowa
thunder *n* মেঘের ডাক megher ḍak
ticket *n* টিকিট ṭikiṭ
tie *vb* বাঁধা bãdha; *n* টাই ṭai
tiger *n* বাঘ ba:gh
tight *adj* কষা kɔsha
time *n* সময় shɔmɔy
tip *n* ডগা ḍɔga
tire *n* চাকা caka
tired *adj* ক্লান্ত klanto, কাহিল kahil
title *n* শিরনাম shironam
today *adv* আজ aj, আজকে ajke
together *adv* একসঙ্গে ekshɔngge
toilet *n* টয়লেট ṭɔyleṭ, পায়খানা paykhana
tomato *n* টোমেটো ṭomeṭo
tomorrow *adv* কালকে kalke, আগামিকাল agamikal
tongue *n* জিব jib
too *adv* ও o
tool *n* যন্ত্র jɔntro
tooth *n* দাঁত dãt

torch *n* টর্চলাইট ṭɔrclaiṭ
totally *adv* সম্পূর্ণ shɔmpurno, একেবারে ekebare
touch *n* স্পর্শ shpɔrsho, *vb* ছোঁয়া chõwa
tourism *n* প্রমোদভ্রমণের ব্যবসা promodbhrɔmoner bæbsha
tourist *n* ভ্রমণকারী bhrɔmonkari
towel *n* গামছা gamcha, তোয়ালে towale
town *n* শহর shɔhor, নগর nɔgor
toy *n* খেলনা khælna
trade *n* বিনিময় binimɔy, ক্রয়-বিক্রয় krɔy-bikrɔy
tradition *n* ঐতিহ্য oitijjo
train *n* রেলগাড়ি relgaṛi
transport *n* যান jan, পরিবহণ poribɔhon
travel *n* ভ্রমণ bhromon
treatment *n* চিকিৎসা cikitsha
tree *n* গাছ gach
trip *n* যাত্রা jatra
trouble *n* ঝামেলা jhamela, অসুবিধা ɔshubidha
trousers *n* প্যান্ট pænṭ
true *adj* সত্য shɔtto, সত্যিকার shottikar
truth *n* সত্যি shotti
try *vb* চেষ্টা করা ceshṭa kɔra
tuberose *n* রজনীগন্ধা rɔjonigɔndha
tube well *n* নলকূপ nɔlkup
turn *vb* ঘোরা ghora
turn down *vb* অগ্রাহ্য করা ɔgrajjo kɔra
turn off *vb* বন্ধ করা bɔndho kɔra
turn on *vb* চালিয়ে দেওয়া caliye deowa
turtle *n* কচ্ছপ kɔcchop, কাছিম kachim
twilight *n* গোধুলি godhuli
twin *n* জমজ jɔmoj
type *n* ধরন dhɔron, রকম rɔkom
typical *adj* বৈশিষ্ট্যমূলক boishistomulok

U

ugly *adj* বিশ্রী bisri, কুৎসিত kutshit
umbrella *n* ছাতা chata, ছাতি chati
unbearable *adj* অসহ্য ɔshojjo
uncle → *see kinship terms (pages 205-207)*
uncommon *adj* অসাধারণ ɔshadharon
under *prep* নিচে nice
understand *vb* বোঝা bojha
uneducated *adj* অশিক্ষিত ɔshikkhito
unemployed *adj* বেকার bekar
unfriendly *adj* অমিশুক ɔmishuk
unhappy *adj* বিষণ্ন bishɔnno, মন খারাপ mon kharap
union *n* সংযোগ shɔngjog, মিলন milon
university *n* বিশ্ববিদ্যালয় bisshobiddalɔy
unknown *adj* অচেনা ɔcena
unnecessary *adj* অপ্রয়োজন ɔproyojon
unsafe *adj* বিপজ্জনক bipojjɔnok
until *prep* পর্যন্ত porjonto
up *adv* উপরের দিকে uporer dike
upset *vb* উলটানো ulṭano, *adj* অস্থির ɔsthir
upside down *adv* উলটা ulṭa
upstairs *adj* উপরতলায় uportɔlay
urgent *adj* জরুরি joruri
use *n* ব্যবহার bæbohar; *vb* ব্যবহার করা bæbohar kɔra
useful *adj* ব্যবহারিক bæboharik
usual *adj* সাধারণ shadharon
usually *adv* সাধারণত shadharonoto

V

vacant *adj* ফাঁকা phãka, খালি khali
vacation *n* ছুটি chuṭi
vaccination *n* টিকা ṭika
vague *adj* অস্পষ্ট ɔshpɔshṭo

valley *n* উপত্যকা upottɔkka
valuable *adj* মূল্যবান mulloban
value *n* মূল্য mullo, দাম da:m
various *adj* নানা nana
vegetable *n* সবজি shobji
vegetarian *adj* নিরামিষ niramish
vehicle *n* গাড়ি gaṛi
very *adv* খুব khub
vest *n* গেঞ্জি genji
victory *n* বিজয় bijɔy
view *n* দৃশ্য drissho
village *n* গ্রাম gram
visa *n* ভিসা bhisa
visit *vb* বেড়ানো beṛano
visitor *n* অতিথি otithi, মেহমান mehoman
vitamin *n* ভিট্যামিন bhiṭamin
voice *n* সুর shur
voluntary *adj* ইচ্ছাজনিত icchajonito
volunteer *n* স্বেচ্ছাকর্মী shecchakormi
vomit *vb* বমি করা bomi kɔra
vote *n* নির্বাচন nirbacon, ভোট bhoṭ
vulture *n* শকুনি shokuni

W

wage *n* বেতন beton
wait *vb* অপেক্ষা করা ɔpekkha kɔra
wake *vb* জাগা jaga
walk *vb* হাঁটা hãṭa
wall *n* দেওয়াল deowal
want *vb* চাওয়া caowa
war *n* যুদ্ধ juddho
warm *adj* গরম gɔrom
warn *vb* সতর্ক করা shɔtɔrko kɔra
wash *vb* ধোয়া dhowa
washerman *n* ধোপা dhopa

waste *n* নষ্ট nɔshṭo
watch *n* ঘড়ি ghoṛi; *vb* নজর রাখা nɔjor rakha
watchman *n* চৌকিদার coukidar
water *n* জল jɔl, পানি pani
water buffalo *n* মহিষ mohish
watermelon *n* তরমুজ tormuj
way *n* পথ pɔth, উপায় upay
weak *adj* দুর্বল durbol
wealth *n* ধন dhɔn
wear *vb* পরা pɔra
weather *n* আবহাওয়া abhaowa
wedding *n* বিয়ে biye, বিবাহ bibaho
week *n* সপ্তাহ shɔptaho
welcome *n* স্বাগতম shagotom
well *adj* ভাল bhalo
west *n* পশ্চিম poshcim
wet *adj* ভিজা bhija, ভিজে bhije
what *pr* কি ki
whatever *adv* যে কোনও je kono
wheat *n* গম gɔm
wheel *n* চাকা caka
when *adv* কখন kɔkhon, কবে kɔbe
where *adv* কোথায় kɔthay
which *pr* কোন kon
white *adj* সাদা shada
who *pr* কে ke
whole *adj* সারা shara, পুরা pura, সমস্ত shomosto
wide *adj* চওড়া cɔoṛa
widow *n* বিধবা bidhoba
wife *n* স্ত্রী stri:, বউ bou
wild *adj* অবাধ্য ɔbaddho
will *n* ইচ্ছা iccha
win *vb* জিতা jita, জয়ী হওয়া jɔyi hɔowa
wind *n* বাতাস batash, হাওয়া haowa
window *n* জানালা janala
wine *n* মদ mɔd

winter *n* শীতকাল shitkal
wisdom *n* বুদ্ধি buddhi
wish *n* ইচ্ছা iccha, কামনা kamona
with *prep* (*in company of*) সঙ্গে shɔngge, সাথে shathe; (*making use of*) দিয়ে diye, নিয়ে niye
without *prep* ছাড়া chaṛa, বিনা bina
woman *n* মহিলা mohila, নারী nari
wood *n* কাঠ kaṭh
word *n* (*uttered sound*) শব্দ shɔbdo; (*statement*) কথা kɔtha
work *n* কাজ kaj; *vb* কাজ করা kaj kɔra
world *n* বিশ্ব bissho, পৃথিবী prithibi, দুনিয়া duniya
worry *n* চিন্তা cinta, দুশ্চিন্তা dushcinta
worth *n* মূল্য mullo
wound *n* ঘা gha
write *vb* লেখা lekha
writer *n* লেখক lekhok
wrong *n* অন্যায় ɔnnay; *adj* ভুল bhu:l

X/Y/Z

x-ray *n* রঞ্জন-রশ্মি rɔnjon-rosshi
yard *n* উঠান uṭhan
year *n* বছর bɔchor
yellow *adj* হলুদ holud, হলদে hɔlde
yes *adv* হ্যাঁ hæ̃
yesterday *adv* গতকাল gɔtokal, কালকে kalke
yet *adv* এখনও ekhono
yogurt *n* দই doi
young *adj* তরুণ torun
zero *n* শূন্য shunno
zoo *n* চিড়িয়াখানা ciṛiyakhana

PHRASEBOOK CONTENTS

GREETINGS, FAREWELLS, THANK YOUS

Muslims greet one another with: **Peace be with you.**
সালাম ওয়ালিকুম।
salam owalikum.

The reply is: ওয়ালিকুম সালাম।
owalikum salam.

Hindu and Christian greeting: নমস্কার nɔmoshkar

Hi! (*Muslim informal*)
আদাব !
adab!

How's things?
কেমন?
kæmon?

How are you?
কেমন আছেন?
kæmon achen?

You are well, I hope?
ভাল আছেন তো?
bhalo achen to?

I am well.
আমি ভাল আছি।
ami bhalo achi.

Not great.
বেশি ভাল নেই।
beshi bhalo nei.

What's new?
কি খবর?
ki khɔbor?

Bye-bye. *(Arabic: God with you)*
খোদা হাফেজ।
khoda haphej.

I'm off.
যাই। *or* যাচ্ছি।
jai. jacchi.

OK, I'm off now.
আচ্ছা আসি।
accha ashi.

See you again.
আবার দেখা হবে।
abar dekha hɔbe.

Stay well.
ভাল থাকবেন।
bhalo thakben.

Come again.
আবার আসবেন।
abar ashben.

Bengalis don't use *please* and *thank you* as much as English-speaking people do. The word for *please* is দয়া করে dɔya kore. The word for *thank you* is ধন্যবাদ dhɔnnobad. It is more usual to express one's appreciation with phrases like:

> আমি খুব খুশি হয়েছি।
> ami khub khushi hoyechi.
> **I am very happy.**
>
> *or*
>
> কষ্ট দিলাম।
> kɔshṭo dilam.
> **I have caused bother.**

Polite requests can be phrased as questions without the use of দয়া করে dɔya kore *please*.

> একটু চা দেবেন?
> ekṭu ca deben?
> **Give me some tea, please?**

MAKING CONTACT

If you want to avoid being swamped by a flood of incomprehensible language, it is a good idea to establish right from the start just how much Bangla you can speak and understand. Here are some useful phrases for doing that.

I can't speak Bangla.
আমি বাংলা বলতে পারি না।
ami bangla bolte pari na.

I can speak a bit of Bangla.
আমি অল্প বাংলা বলতে পারি।
ami ɔlpo bangla bolte pari.

Speak slowly.
আস্তে আস্তে বলুন।
aste aste bolun.

Can you speak English?
ইংরেজি বলতে পারেন?
ingreji bolte paren?

I have just arrived.
আমি নতুন এসেছি।
ami notun eshechi.

I am learning Bangla.
আমি বাংলা শিখছি।
ami bangla shikhchi.

I want to learn Bangla.
আমি বাংলা শিখতে চাই।
ami bangla shikhte cai.

I have come here to learn Bangla.
আমি এখানে বাংলা শিখতে এসেছি।
ami ekhane bangla shikhte eshechi.

Don't speak English with me.
আমার সঙ্গে ইংরেজি বলবেন না।
amar sɔngge ingreji bolben na.

I need to speak Bangla.
আমার বাংলা বলা দরকার।
amar bangla bɔla dɔrkar.

I want to learn quickly.
আমি তাড়াতাড়ি শিখতে চাই।
ami taṛataṛi shikhte cai.

Can you help me?
আপনি আমাকে সাহায্য করবেন?
apni amake shahajjo korben?

Will you teach me?
আপনি আমাকে শেখাবেন?
apni amake shekhaben?

I don't know.
আমি জানি না।
ami jani na.

I don't understand.
আমি বুঝি না।
ami bujhi na.

I can't understand anything.
আমি কিছু বুঝতে পারছি না।
ami kichu bujhte parchi na.

I won't be able to remember all this.
এসব মনে রাখতে পারব না।
eshɔb mone rakhte parbo na.

What did you say?
কি বলেছেন?
ki bolechen?

Say (it) again. / Repeat.
আবার বলুন।
abar bolun.

The pronunciation is very difficult.
উচ্চারণটা খুব কঠিন।
uccaronṭa khub koṭhin.

What is this word?
এই শব্দটা কি?
ei shɔbdoṭa ki?

I can't read Bangla.
আমি বাংলা পড়তে পারি না।
ami bangla poṛte pari na.

What is this?
এটা কি?
eṭa ki?

What are these?
এগুলো কি?
egulo ki?

What's that in Bangla?
এটা বাংলায় কি?
eṭa banglay ki?

What does this mean?
এটার মানে কি?
eṭar mane ki?

What should I say?
কি বলব?
ki bolbo?

Please correct my mistakes.
আমার ভুলগুলো ঠিক করে দেন।
amar bhulgulo ṭhik kore den.

YES AND NO

Yes. হ্যাঁ hæ̃ *or* জি ji:

No. না na *or* জিনা jina

There is ... ... আছে ... ache

There is time. সময় আছে। shomoy ache.

Is there any tea? চা আছে? ca ache?

There isn't ... ... নেই ... nei

There is no one here. এখানে কেউ নেই। ekhane keu nei.

No problem. অসুবিধা নেই। oshubidha nei.

Right. ঠিক। ṭhi:k.

OK. আচ্ছা। acchha.

OK, all right. ঠিক আছে। ṭhi:k ache.

Of course. নিশ্চয়। nishcɔy.

Not at all. মোটেই না। moṭe-i na

I don't know. আমি জানি না। ami jani na.

INTRODUCTIONS

Who are you?
আপনি কে? apni ke?

What's your name?
আপনার নাম কি?
apnar nam ki?

> **My name is Helen.**
> আমার নাম হেলেন।
> amar nam helen.

What should I call you?
আপনাকে কি বলে ডাকবো?
apnake ki bole ḍakbo?

Which country are you from?
আপনি কোন দেশের মানুষ?
apni kon desher manush?

Where are you from?
আপনার দেশ কোথায়?
apnar desh kothay?

> **I come from America/England.**
> আমার দেশ আমেরিকা / ইংল্যান্ড।
> amar desh amerika/inglænḍ.

How long will you stay?
কতদিন থাকবেন?
kɔtodin thakben?

> **I will stay for ... .**
> আমি ... থাকব।
> ami ... thakbo.

two months	দুই মাস	dui ma:sh
three weeks	তিন সপ্তাহ	tin shɔptaho
five days	পাঁচ দিন	pãc di:n
a little while	কিছুক্ষণ	kichukkhɔn

Where are you staying?
কোথায় থাকেন?
kothay thaken?

I am staying in the hostel.
আমি হস্টেলে থাকি।
ami hosṭele thaki.

I am staying with my friend.
আমি আমার বন্ধুর বাসায় থাকি।
ami amar bondhur bashay thaki.

How do you like it? ***or*** **How do you (does it) feel?**
কেমন লাগে?
kæmon lage?

How do you like Bangladesh/Kolkata?
বাংলাদেশ / কলকাতা কেমন লাগে?
bangladesh/kolkata kæmon lage?

It still feels strange.
এখনও অচেনা লাগে।
ekhono ɔcena lage.

I like it very much.
খুব ভাল লাগে।
khub bhalo lage.

I have never been here before.
আমি এর আগে কখনও আসিনি।
ami er age kɔkhono ashini.

Why have you come here?
আপনি কেন এখানে এসেছেন?
apni kæno ekhane eshechen?

What (work) do you do?
আপনি কি (কাজ) করেন?
apni ki (kaj) koren?

What are you doing here?
আপনি এখানে কি করছেন?
apni ekhane ki korchen?

I am a student (*male*).
আমি ছাত্র।
ami chatro.
I am a student here (*female*).
আমি এখানে ছাত্রী।
ami ekhane chatri.

I am a doctor.
আমি ডাক্তার।
ami ḍaktar.

I am a volunteer.
আমি স্বেচ্ছাসেবক।
ami shecchhashebok.

I have come to work.
আমি কাজ করতে এসেছি।
ami kaj korte eshechi.

I have come for a visit.
আমি বেড়াতে এসেছি।
ami beṛate eshechi.

Will you introduce me to them?
আমাকে তাদের সঙ্গে পরিচয় করিয়ে দেবেন?
amake tader sɔngge poricɔy koriye deben?

How old are you?
আপনার বয়স কত?
apnar bɔyosh kɔto?

I am ... years old.
আমার বয়স ...।
amar bɔyosh ... .
20 বিশ bi:sh
25 পঁচিশ põcish
(*See more numbers on pages 210-211*)

Are you married?
আপনার বিয়ে হয়েছে?
apnar biye hoyeche?

No, I'm not married.
না, আমার বিয়ে হয়নি।
na, amar biye hɔy ni.

Yes, I am married.
হ্যাঁ, আমার বিয়ে হয়েছে।
hæ̃, amar biye hoyeche.

Do you have children?
অপনার ছেলেমেয়ে আছে?
apnar chelemeye ache?

Don't you have children?
ছেলেমেয়ে নেই?
chelemeye nei?

Yes, I have two sons.
হ্যাঁ, আমার দুইটা ছেলে।
hæ̃, amar duiṭa chele.

Yes, I have two daughters.
হ্যাঁ, আমার দুইটা মেয়ে।
hæ̃, amar duiṭa meye.

No, I don't have children.
না, আমার ছেলেমেয়ে নেই।
na, amar chelemeye nei.

No, I am still too young.
না, আমার এখনও বয়স অল্প।
na, amar ekhono bɔyosh ɔlpo.

Do you have brothers and sisters?
আপনার ভাইবোন আছে?
apnar bhaibon ache?

I have three brothers and sisters.
আমার তিন ভাইবোন।
amar tin bhaibon.

Where are your parents?
আপনার মা-বাবা কোথায়?
apnar ma-baba kothay?

My parents are back at home.
আমার মা-বাবা দেশে।
amar ma-baba deshe.

DIRECTIONS

where?	**which way?**
কোথায়?	কোন দিকে?
kothay?	kon dike?

straight
সোজা
shoja

to the right
ডান দিকে *or* ডানে *or* ডান হাতে
ḍan dike ḍane ḍan hate

to the left
বাঁ দিকে *or* বাঁয়ে *or* বাঁ হাতে
bã dike bãye bã hate

straight ahead / in front
সামনে
shamne

behind / at the back
পিছনে
pichone

this way	**that way**
এই দিকে	ওই দিকে
ei dike	oi dike

very far
অনেক দূরে
ɔnek dure

a little way / some distance
কিছু দূর
kichu dur

very close
খুব কাছে
khub kache

I will go.
আমি যাব।
ami jabo.

You will go.
আপনি যাবেন।
apni jaben.

I will get off.
আমি নামবো।
ami nambo.

How do I get there?
আমি ওখানে কি করে যাব?
ami okhane ki kore jabo?

Will you take me with you?
আপনি আমাকে নিয়ে যাবেন?
apni amake niye jaben?

Let me get off here.
এখানে আমাকে নামিয়ে দেন।
ekhane amake namiye den.

Which way are you going?
কোন দিকে যাচ্ছেন?
kon dike jacchen?

Not this way, surely!
এই দিকে না তো!
ei dike na to!

I will walk from here.
এখান থেকে হেঁটে যাব।
ekhan theke hẽṭe jabo.

Don't you know the road?
রাস্তা চেনেন না?
rasta cenen na?

Can you ask someone?
কাউকে জিজ্ঞাস করে নেন?
kauke jiggash kore nen?

Wait a minute.
এক মিনিট।
ek miniṭ.

Let me have a look.
একটু দেখে নেই।
ektu dekhe nei.

I (don't) know this road.
আমি রাস্তাটা চিনি (না)।
ami rastaṭa cini (na).

I (don't) know this area.
আমি এই এলাকাটা চিনি (না)।
ami ei elakaṭa cini (na).

I (don't) know the place.
আমি জায়গাটা চিনি না।
ami jaygaṭa cini (na).

How do I find ...?
... কেমন করে পাব?
... kæmon kore pabo?

What's the road number?
রাস্তার নম্বরটা কত?
rastar nombor koto?

address ঠিকানা ṭhikana
name of the hotel হোটেলের নাম hoṭeler nam

TRAVEL AND TRANSPORTATION

LOCAL TRAVEL (Dhaka and Kolkata)

When you are using any kind of public transport (Rickshaw, CNG, tempo, bus, etc.) it is good to know what kind of fare to expect. Rickshaw drivers are usually reluctant to name a price upfront (দেন den **give!**) so the best thing is for you to name a price and negotiate. People will not respect you if you pay way above the odds, though an extra five *Taka* is usually appreciated.

Cycle-rickshaws

Cycle-rickshaws for shorter distances, can be hailed in the street:

এই, রিকশা
ei riksha
hello, rickshaw

ওই, খালি
oi khali
hi, empty

Nowadays, because of the increase in traffic, rickshaws are not allowed on the main roads of Dhaka during the day, so you may have to walk a little bit to find one. However, they are still one of the best ways to get around and the only vehicles that can go through when roads turn into rivers in the monsoons. There are no cycle rickshaws in the center of Kolkata and hand-pulled rickshaws (quite apart from their exploitative aspects) are no faster than walking.

A typical conversation goes like this:

Will you go?
যাবেন?
jaben?

Yes, where to?
হ্যাঁ, কোথায় যাব?
hæ̃, kothay jabo?

Take me to Gulshan market.
গুলশান বাজারে নিয়ে যান।
gulshan bajare niye jan.

How much?
ভাড়া কত?
bhaṛa kɔto?

Twenty Taka.
বিশ টাকা।
bish ṭaka.

No, that's too much.
না, এটা বেশি।
na, eṭa beshi.

How much will you pay?
কত দেবেন?
kɔto deben?

I'll give you fifteen.
আমি পনেরো টাকা দেব।
ami pɔnero ṭaka debo.

OK. Get on.
ঠিক আছে, উঠেন।
ṭhik ache, uṭhen.

CNG (formerly baby-taxis) in Dhaka, auto-rickshaws in Kolkata

These are motorized scooters with the driver sitting in front and room for up to three passengers behind him. They are very versatile and can squeeze through where cars won't go. Fares are cheaper than for a taxi. They can take you anywhere within the town. It is very important to negotiate a price beforehand and to have the right money. Many drivers will be keen to ferry you around all day, so be clear from the start if you just want to be dropped off somewhere.

Taxis

There are plenty of taxis in Dhaka and Kolkata. You can hail them in the street but you can also pick them up from designated taxi stands. It is good to have some idea of the distance you are going and of the approximate fare before you start your journey. Many taxis have a meter running but this system does not always work. Places and addresses are not always easy to find and drivers may not know them any better than you do, even if they think they do. If you run into problems, the best thing to do is to stop and ask for directions.

Buses

These have fixed routes. They are good and cheap if you are sure of where you are going, and the fares are fixed. There is usually segregated seating for women on buses. Buses are often rather crowded so it is not a good idea to take a lot of luggage with you. For obvious reasons, it is not a good idea to use buses when you don't know where you are going.

What time will the car/bus go?
গাড়ি কোন সময় ছাড়বে?
gaṛi kon shɔmɔy chaṛbe?

What time will I get there?
কোন সময় পৌঁছাব?
kon shɔmɔy põuchabo?

Is it possible to go by rickshaw?
রিকশায় যাওয়া যায়?
rikshay jaowa jay?

> **No, it's much too far.**
> না, দূর অনেক বেশি।
> na, dur ɔnek beshi.

I don't have much time.
আমার বেশি সময় নেই।
amar beshi shɔmɔy nei.

Can we hire a car?
একটা গাড়ি ভাড়া নিতে পারি?
ekṭa gaṛi bhaṛa nite pari

How much is/are the ticket(s)?
টিকেটের দাম কত?
ṭikeṭer dam kɔto?

Where is the station?
ইস্টেশন কোথায়?
isteshon kothay?

At what time do I have to be at the airport?
বিমান বন্দরে কোন সময় থাকতে হবে?
biman bɔndore kon shomoy thakte hɔbe?

How much longer?
আর কত দেরি?
ar kɔto deri?

Is there any food available around here?
এখানে কি কোনও খাবার জিনিস পাওয়া যায়?
ekhane ki kono khabar jinish paowa jay?

When will the boat come?
নৌকা কোন সময় আসবে?
nouka kon shomoy ashbe?

LONG-DISTANCE TRAVEL (bus, train, and plane)

Bangladesh

For long distance bus journeys (country-wide) it is sensible to book in advance and to tell the driver where you want to go. A bus-trip overland, say from Dhaka to Rajshahi or from Dhaka to Chittagong, is a memorable experience in itself and knowing some Bangla is essential. Once the crowds, traffic and pollution of Dhaka is left behind, Bangladesh reveals itself as a country of great charm and beauty.

West Bengal
Anyone travelling in West Bengal should experience a train journey. The two main Kolkata railway stations (Howrah and Sealdah) are memorable places to visit with their bustle of activity, great variety of people, whole families with all their worldly goods packed up in colorful bundles and all the excitement of traveling.

Where can I buy a ticket?
টিকিট কিনব কোথায়?
ṭikiṭ kinbo kothay?

Where does this bus/train go?
এই বাস/ট্রেন কোথায় যায়?
ei bas/ṭren kothay jay?

Is this the bus/train to Rajshahi?
এটা কি রাজশাহীর বাস/ট্রেন?
eṭa ki rajshahir bas/ṭren?

When does the bus/train leave?
বাস/ট্রেন কোন সময় ছাড়বে?
bas/ṭren kon sɔmɔy chaṛbe?

I will take ... ticket(s).
আমি ... টিকিট নেব।
ami ... ṭikiṭ nebo.

one	একটা	ækṭa
two	দুইটা	duiṭa
three	তিনটা	tinṭa

How long will it take to get to Khulna/Howrah?
খুলনা/হাওরা যেতে কতক্ষণ লাগবে?
khulna/howra jete kɔtokkhɔn lagbe?

Where does the bus leave from?
বাস কোথা থেকে যাবে?
bas kotha theke jabe?

Is this the bus-stand?
এটা কি বাস স্ট্যান্ড?
eṭa ki bas stænḍ?

Which platform does the train leave from?
ট্রেন কোন প্ল্যাটফোর্ম থেকে ছাড়বে?
ṭren kon plæṭform theke chaṛbe?

What is the delay?
দেরি হচ্ছে কেন?
deri hocche kæno?

Can I have a different seat?
অন্য একটা সিট দিতে পারেন?
ɔnno ekṭa siṭ dite paren?

This is my seat.
এটা আমার সিট।
eṭa amar siṭ.

Will you tell me where to get off?
কোথায় নামতে হবে বলবেন?
kothay namte hɔbe bolben?

Where can I put my bag?
আমার ব্যাগ কোথায় রাখব?
amar bæg kothay rakhbo?

Does the train stop in Bonpara?
ট্রেনটা কি বনপাড়ায় থামবে?
ṭrenṭa ki bɔnpaṛa thambe?

We will go by plane.
আমরা বিমানে যাব।
amra bimane jabo.

airport বিমান বন্দর biman bondor
train station ইস্টেশন isṭeshon

ACCOMMODATIONS

English is widely understood in the bigger hotels in Kolkata and Dhaka. In smaller hotels and outside the main cities a mixture of Bangla and English is the norm.

I am looking for accommodations for tonight.
আমি আজ রাতের জন্যে থাকার জায়গা খুঁজছি।
ami aj rater jonne thakar jayga khũjchi.

Do you have rooms available?
আপনাদের রুম খালি আছে?
apnader rum khali ache?

I have booked a room.
আমার একটা রুম বুক করা আছে।
amar ækṭa rum buk kɔra ache.

Can you recommend another hotel?
অন্য একটা হোটেল সুপারিশ করতে পারেন?
ɔnno ekṭa hoṭel shuparish korte paren?

I want a single/double room.
আমি একটা সিঙ্গেল/ ডবল রুম নেব।
ami ekṭa singol/ḍɔbol rum nebo.

How much is it ...?
... ভাড়া কত?
... bhaṛa kɔto?

for one night এক রাতের জন্যে æk rater jonne
for two people দুজনের জন্যে dujɔner jonne
for a week এক সপ্তাহের জন্যে æk shɔptaher jonne
with food খাবার দিয়ে khabar diye
without food খাবার ছাড়া khabar chaṛa

Does the room have ...?
রুমে ... আছে?
rume ... ache?

a fan পাখা pakha
a lock তালা tala
a bathroom বাথরুম bathrum

hot water গরম পানি gɔrom pani
a mosquito net মশারি mɔshari
room service রুম সার্ভিস rum sarbhis
laundry service কাপড় ধোয়ার ব্যবস্থা kapoṛ dhowar bæbostha
electricity বিদ্যুৎ biddut, কারেন্ট karenṭ
air conditioning এ সি e si
a TV টিভি ṭibhi
Internet ইন্টারনেট inṭarneṭ

What time is ...?
... কোন সময়?
... kon sɔmɔy?
breakfast সকালের নাস্তা shɔkaler nasta
lunch লান্চ lanc
dinner রাতের খাবার rater khabar
check-in চেক-ইন cek-in
check-out চেক-আউট cek-auṭ

What time will the power come back on?
বিদ্যুৎ আবার কোন সময় আসবে?
biddut abar kon shɔmɔy ashbe?

Can you look after my ...?
আমার ... রেখে দিতে পারেন?
amar ... rekhe dite paren?
luggage মাল mal
passport পাসপোর্ট pasporṭ
money টাকা ṭaka

Can you give me a wake-up call?
আমাকে সকালে ডাক দিতে পারেন?
amake shɔkale ḍak dite paren?

I would like ... .
আমাকে ... দিতে পারেন।
amake ... dite paren.
a different room অন্য একটা ঘর ɔnno ækṭa ghɔr

a blanket একটা কম্বল ækṭa kɔmbol
a flashlight একটা টর্চলাইট ækṭa ṭorclait
another pillow আর একটা বালিশ ar ækṭa balish
a bottle of water এক বোতল পানি / জল æk botol pani/jɔl
a glass একটা গেলাস ækṭa gelash
soap সাবান shaban
a towel একটা তোয়ালে ækṭa towale
toilet paper টয়লেট পেপার ṭɔyleṭ pepar
a newspaper একটা খবরের কাগজ ækṭa khɔborer kagoj
a map একটা মানচিত্র ækṭa mancitro

FOOD AND DRINK

The same verb খাওয়া khaowa is used for eating, drinking, and any other type of oral consumption, eg. ওষুধ খাওয়া oshudh khaowa *take medicine*; বাতাস খাওয়া batash khaowa *get some air*; সিগারেট খাওয়া sigareṭ khaowa *smoke*; চুমু খাওয়া cumu khaowa *kiss,* etc.

TEA AND COFFEE

Will you have some tea?
চা খাবেন?
ca khaben?

> **Yes, I'll have some.**
> হ্যাঁ, খাব।
> hæ̃, khabo.

Do you want milk and sugar?
দুধ চিনি দেব?
dudh cini debo?

> **No, just milk.**
> না, শুধু দুধ দেন।
> na, shudhu dudh den.

> **No, I'll have it black.**
> না, লাল চা খাব।
> na, lal ca khabo.

Should I make some lemon tea?
লেবু চা বানাই?
lebu ca banai?

> **I don't drink tea.**
> আমি চা খাই না।
> ami ca khai na.

> **Lemon tea is delicious.**
> লেবু চা খুব মজা।
> lebu ca khub mɔja.

Is there any coffee?
কফি আছে?
kophi ache?

> **Of course, I'll get it.**
> অবশ্য, দিচ্ছি।
> ɔbossho, dicchhi.

Just give me a glass of water.
আমাকে শুধু এক গেলাস পানি দেন।
amake shudhu æk gelash pani den.

DINNER

I am very hungry.
আমার খুব খিদা পেয়েছে।
amar khub khida peyeche.

Give me more rice, please.
আরও ভাত দেন।
aro bhat den.

Don't give me a lot.
আমাকে বেশি দেবেন না।
amake beshi deben na.

I'll just have a little.
আমি অল্প খাব।
ami ɔlpo khabo.

Do you want some meat?
মাংস দেব?
mangsho debo?

> **No, I don't eat meat.**
> না, আমি মাংস খাই না।
> na, ami mangsho khai na.

> **I am a vegetarian.**
> আমি নিরামিষ খাই।
> ami niramish khai.

Can I have a bit more sauce?
আর একটু ঝোল দেন।
ar ekṭu jhol den.

The fish is delicious.
মাছটা খুব মজা।
machṭa khub mɔja.

Can I have some salt, please?
একটু নুন/লবণ দিতে পারেন?
ekṭu nun/lɔbon dite paren?

Do you want some more?
আরও নেবেন?
aro neben?

> **No, I am full.**
> না, না, আমার পেট ভরে গেছে।
> na, na, amar peṭ bhore geche.
>
> **I would like more vegetables.**
> সবজি আরও খেতে পারি।
> shobji aro khete pari.

What are these?
এগুলো কি?
egulo ki?

I can't eat chilies.
আমি মরিচ খেতে পারি না।
ami moric khete pari na.

The food is too spicy for me.
আমার জন্যে ঝাল বেশি হয়েছে।
amar jonne jhal beshi hoyeche.

The curry is very tasty.
তরকারি খুব স্বাদ হয়েছে।
tɔrkari khub shad hoyeche.

I enjoyed your cooking very much.
আপনার রান্না খুব ভাল লেগেছে।
apnar ranna khub bhalo legeche.

EATING OUT

We are looking for a nice restaurant.
আমরা ভাল একটা রেস্টরাঁ খুঁজছি।
amra bhalo ækṭa resṭorã khũjchi.

I want to reserve a table for tonight.
আজ রাতের খাবরের একটা টেবিল বুক করতে চাই।
a:j rater khabarer ækṭa ṭebil buk korte cai.

We need a table for six people.
ছয়জনের জন্যে একটা টেবিল লাগবে।
chɔyjɔner jonne ækṭa ṭebil lagbe.

I'm sorry but we won't have space tonight.
আমি দুঃখিত আজ রাতে জায়গা হবে না।
ami dukhito a:j rate jayga hɔbe na.

We can arrange it for tomorrow.
কালকের জন্যে ব্যবস্থা করা যাবে।
kalker jonne bæbostha kɔra jabe.

Can I see the menu?
মেনিউটা দেখতে পারব?
meniuṭa dekhte parbo?

Do you have vegetarian food?
নিরামিষ আছে?
niramish ache?

What kinds of drinks do you serve?
কি রকম পানীয় আছে?
ki rɔkom paniyo ache?

Can we have just water please?
শুধু পানি/জল দিলে হবে।
shudhu pani/jɔl dile hɔbe.

I don't want any ice.
বরফ দেবেন না।
bɔroph deben na.

Where can I wash my hands?
হাত ধুব কোথায়?
ha:t dhubo kothay?

Can we order now?
এখন অর্ডার দেব?
ækhon ɔrḍar debo?

Is the food very spicy?
খাবারটা কি খুব ঝাল?
khabarṭa ki khub jhal?

How long will the food take?
খাবার তৈরি করতে কতক্ষণ লাগবে?
khabar toiri korte kɔtokkhɔn lagbe?

We are waiting for someone else.
আমরা আর একজনের জন্যে দেরি করছি।
amra ar ækjɔner jonne deri korchi.

What kind of meat is this?
এটা কিসের মাংস?
eṭa kisher mangsho?

Can I have this without ...?
এটা ... ছাড়া পাওয়া যায়?
eṭa ... chaṛa paowa jay?

chili কাঁচা মরিচ kãca moric
garlic রসুন roshun
milk দুধ dudh
nuts বাদাম badam
oil তেল tel
onion পেঁয়াজ pẽyaj
salt নুন nun; লবণ lɔbon

Could you bring ..., please?
... দিতে পারেন?
... dite paren?

the menu মেনিউটা meniuṭa
the bill বিলটা bilṭa
a fork একটা কাটা চামচ ækṭa kaṭa camoc
some more rice আর একটু ভাত ar ekṭu bha:t
another plate আর একটা থালা ar ækṭa thala
a glass একটা গেলাস ækṭa gelash
a clean spoon পরিষ্কার একটা চামচ porishkar ækṭa camoc
an extra chair আর একটা চেয়ার ar ækṭa ceyar

This is ....
এটা ... ।
eṭa ....

for two people দুজনের জন্যে dujoner jonne
too much বেশি beshi
very tasty খুব মজার khub mɔjar
not hot গরম নয় gɔrom nɔy
not edible খাওয়া যায় না khaowa jay na

This is too spicy.
এটার ঝাল বেশি।
eṭar jhal beshi.

Can you heat this up again?
এটা আবার গরম দিতে পারেন?
eṭa abar gɔrom dite paren?

Do you accept credit cards?
ক্রেডিট কার্ড নেবেন?
kreḍiṭ karḍ neben?

Here is a tip for you.
এই যে আপনার বকশিশ।
ei je apnar bokshish.

We will come again.
আবার আসব একদিন।
abar ashbo ækdin.

Essential Foods

beef গরুর মাংস gorur mangsho
Note: Hindus don't eat beef.
biscuit বিস্কুট biskuṭ
bread রুটি ruṭi
chicken মুর্গির মাংস murgir mangsho
coffee কফি kophi
egg ডিম ḍim
fish মাছ mach
fruit ফল phɔl
honey মধু modhu
lamb খাসির মাংস khashir mangsho
lentil ডাল ḍal
meat মাংস mangsho
milk দুধ dudh
oil তেল tel
pork শূকরের মাংস shukorer mangsho
Note: Muslims don't eat pork.
prawns চিংড়ি মাছ cingṛi mach
rice (cooked) ভাত bhat
salt লবণ, নুন lɔbon, nun
sugar চিনি cini
sweets মিষ্টি mishṭi
tea চা ca
vegetables সবজি shobji

Fruit, Vegetables, Spices

apple আপেল apel
banana কলা kɔla
bay leaf তেজপাতা tejpata
bean (broad) সীম shi:m

bean (green) বরবটি bɔrboṭi
berry জাম jam
cabbage বাঁধাকপি bãdhakopi
cardamom এলাচ elac
carrot গাজর gajor
cauliflower ফুলকপি phulkopi
chili মরিচ moric
cinnamon দারচিনি darcini
clove লবঙ্গ lɔbonggo
coconut নারিকেল narikel
coriander ধনিয়া dhoniya
corn ভুট্টা bhuṭṭa
cucumber শসা shɔsha
cumin জিরা jira
custard apple আতাফল ataphɔl
date খেজুর khejur
eggplant বেগুন begun
fig ডুমুর ḍumur
fruit ফল phɔl
garlic রসুন roshun
ginger আদা ada
gourd লাউ lau
green chili কাঁচা মরিচ kãca moric
green coconut ডাব ḍa:b
green vegetables শাক সবজি sha:k shobji
guava পেয়ারা peyara
jackfruit কাঁঠাল kãṭhal
jasmine জুঁই jũi
jujube বরই bɔroi
lady's finger (okra) ঢেঁড়স ḍhæ̃ṛosh
lemon লেবু lebu
lychee লিচু licu
mango আম a:m
melon ফুটি phuṭi
mint পুদিনা pudina
mixed spices গরম মসলা gɔrom mɔshla

mustard সরিষা shorisha
nut বাদাম badam
nutmeg জায়ফল jayphɔl
okra ঢেঁড়স ḍhæ̃ṛosh
olive জলপাই jɔlpai
onion পেঁয়াজ pẽyaj, পিয়াজ piyaj
orange কমলা kɔmla
papaya পেঁপে pẽpe
pea কলাই kɔlai, মটর mɔṭor
pear নাসপাতি nashpati
pepper গোল মরিচ gol moric
pineapple আনারস anarɔsh
pomegranate ডালিম ḍalim
pomelo জামবুরা jambura
potato আলু alu
pumpkin কুমড়া kumṛa
radish মূলা mula
raisin কিশমিশ kismis
seed বীচি bici
sesame তিল til
snakebean পটোল pɔṭol
snakegourd চিচিঙ্গা cicingga
spice মসলা mɔshla
spices, mixed গরম মসলা gɔrom mɔshla
spinach পালং শাক palong sha:k
sugarcane আখ akh
sweet potato মিষ্টি আলু mishṭi alu
tamarind তেঁতুল tẽtul
tomato টোমেটো ṭomeṭo
turmeric হলুদ holud
turnip শালগম shalgɔm
vegetable সবজি shobji
watermelon তরমুজ tormuj
wood-apple বেল bel

SIGHTSEEING AND SHOPPING

What is there to see around here?
এই এলাকায় কি কি দেখা যায়?
ei elakay ki ki dækha jay?

There is a temple close by.
খুব কাছে একটা মন্দির আছে।
khub kache ækṭa mondir ache.

What time does it open/close?
কোন সময় খোলে/বন্ধ হয়?
kon sɔmɔy khole/bɔndho hɔy?

It's open all day.
সারাদিন খোলা।
sharadin khola.

Which way is it?
এখান থেকে কোন দিকে?
ekhan theke kon dike?

Go straight along this road.
এই রাস্তায় সোজা যান।
ei rastay soja jan.

Can I walk from here?
এখান থেকে কি হেঁটে যাওয়া যায়?
ekhan theke ki hẽṭe jaowa jay?

Yes, it'll take 10 minutes.
হ্যাঁ, দশ মিনিট লাগবে।
hæ̃, dɔsh miniṭ lagbe.

What is this building?
এই দালানটা কি?
ei dalanṭa ki?

This is a ... এটা... eṭa...
bridge ব্রিজ brij, সেতু shetu
church গির্জা girja

mosque মসজিদ moshjid
museum জাদুঘর jadughɔr
observatory মানমন্দির manmodir
palace প্রাসাদ prashad
temple মন্দির mondir
university বিশ্ববিদ্যালয় bisshobiddalɔy
zoo চিড়িয়াখানা ciṛiyakhana

Should I take off my shoes?
জুতা খুলব?
juta khulbo?

Yes, shoes have to be taken off.
হ্যাঁ, জুতা খুলতে হবে।
hæ̃, juta khulte hɔbe.

Can I take my bag in?
আমার ব্যাগ নিয়ে যেতে পারি?
amar bæg niye jete pari?

Leave the bag here.
ব্যাগটা এখানে রেখে যান।
bægṭa ekhane rekhe jan.

Can I take photographs?
ছবি তুলতে পারব?
chobi tulte parbo?

It is forbidden to take photos.
এখানে ছবি তোলা নিষেধ।
ekhane chobi tola nishedh.

Is there a guide?
কোনও গাইড আছে?
kono gaid ache?

Can we go into the garden?
আমরা কি বাগানে ঢুকতে পারব?
amra ki bagane ḍhukte parbo?

Where can I buy ...?
... কোথায় কিনতে পাওয়া যায়?
... kothay kinte paowa jay?

clothes কাপড়-চোপড় kapoṛ- copoṛ
furniture আসবাব ashbab
jewelry গয়না gɔyna
music গান-বাজনা gan-bajna
shoes জুতা juta
toys খেলনা khælna

What will you have?
কি নেবেন?
ki neben?

How much is it?
দাম কত?
dam kɔto?

less কম kɔm
a lot / too much বেশি beshi

That's far too expensive.
দাম অনেক বেশি।
dam ɔnek beshi.

How much will you take?
কত নেবেন?
kɔto neben?

I will take four yards.
আমি চার গজ নেব।
ami car gɔj nebo.

How many will you have?
কয়টা নেবেন?
kɔyṭa neben?

I'll take six.
আমি ছয়টা নেব।
ami chhɔyṭa nebo.

Give me two more.
আরও দুইটা দেন।
aro duita den.

Which one(s) do you want?
কোনটা । কোনগুলো নেবেন?
konṭa /kongulo neben?

this one	**these ones**	**not this one**
এটা	এগুলো	এটা না
eṭa	egulo	eṭa na

What else?
আর কি?
ar ki?

Nothing else.
আর কিছু না।
ar kichu na.

Do you have postcards?
পোস্টকার্ড আছে?
posṭkarḍ ache?

No, we don't.	**Yes, we do.**
না, নেই।	হ্যাঁ, আছে।
na, nei.	hæ̃, ache.

Is there a bookshop here?
এখানে বইয়ের দোকান আছে?
ekhane boiyer dokan ache?

I don't need anything else.
আর কিছু লাগবে না।
ar kichu lagbe na.

COMMUNICATION AND MONEY

Where can I change some money?
টাকা কোথায় বদলাতে পারব?
ṭaka kothay bɔdlate parbo?

I need to go to a bank.
আমাকে ব্যাংকে যেতে হবে।
amake bængke jete hɔbe.

Where is the nearest ATM?
কাছে একটা এ টি এম কোথায়?
kache ækṭa e ṭi em kothay?

Can I withdraw money here?
এখানে টাকা তুলতে পারব?
ekhane ṭaka tulte parbo?

Do you accept traveler's checks?
আপনারা ট্র্যাভেলের চেক নেবেন?
apnara ṭræbheler cek neben?

Can you give me some change, please?
আমাকে একটু খুচরা টাকা দেওয়া যাবে?
amake ekṭu khucra ṭaka deowa jabe?

I need the money quickly.
টাকাটা আমার খুব তাড়াতাড়ি দরকার।
ṭakaṭa amar khub taṛataṛi dɔrkar.

There is no rush.
কোনও তাড়া নেই।
kono taṛa nei.

Where is the post office?
পোস্টাপিসটা কোথায়?
posṭapisṭa kothay?

Where can I post/mail my letters?
চিঠি কোথায় জমা দেব?
ciṭhi kothay jɔma debo?

What time does the post office open?
পোস্টাপিস কোন সময় খোলে?
posṭapis kon shɔmɔy khole?

I need to send a telegram/fax.
একটা টেলিগ্রাম/ফ্যাক্স পাঠাতে হবে।
ekṭa ṭeligram/phæks paṭhate hɔbe.

Is there any Internet here?
এখানে কি ইন্টার্নেট আছে?
ekhane ki inṭarneṭ ache?

I need to charge my cell phone.
আমার মোবাইলে চার্জ দিতে হবে।
amar mobaile carj dite hɔbe.

Can I make a phone call from here?
এখানে ফোন করতে পারি?
ekhane phon korte pari?

Is it possible to phone abroad?
বিলাতে কি ফোন করা যায়?
bilate ki phon kɔra jay?

I've been cut off.
লাইনটা কেটে গেছে।
lainṭa keṭe geche.

Where can I make some photocopies?
ফোটোকপি করা যাবে কোথায়?
phoṭokopi kɔra jabe kothay?

NEEDS AND EMOTIONS

How do you like ...?
... কেমন লাগে?
... kæmon lage?

Bangladesh বাংলাদেশ bangladesh
Kolkata কলকাতা kolkata
the town শহরটা shɔhorṭa
the village গ্রামটা gra:mṭa

very nice খুব সুন্দর। khub shundor.
I like it. ভাল লাগে। bhalo lage.
I don't like it. ভাল লাগে না। bhalo lage na.

I feel sad.
আমার মন খারাপ।
amar mon kharap.

I feel hungry.
আমার খিদা পেয়েছে।
amar khida peyeche.

The heat is making me exhausted.
গরমের জন্যে কাহিল লাগছে।
gɔromer jonne kahil lagche.

I miss ... .
... কথা মনে পড়ছে।
... kɔtha mone poṛche.

my country দেশের desher
home বাড়ির baṛir
parents মা-বাবার ma-babar
children বাচ্চাদের baccader
husband স্বামীর shamir
wife বউয়ের bouyer
friends বন্ধুদের bondhuder

I would like to ... .
আমি ... চাই।
ami ... cai.

be alone for a bit
একটু একা থাকতে
ekṭu æka thakte

go somewhere else
অন্য কোথাও যেতে
onno kothao jete

eat something
কিছু খেতে
kichu khete

go to bed
শুতে
shute

stay with you
তোমার সঙ্গে থাকতে
tomar shɔngge thakte

go home
বাসায় যেতে
bashay jete

go for a walk
একটু হেঁটে যেতে
ekṭu hẽṭe jete

talk to them
তাদের সঙ্গে কথা বলতে
tader shɔngge kɔtha bolte

Can you explain to me?
আমাকে বুঝিয়ে দিতে পারেন?
amake bujhiye dite paren?

I can't remember.
মনে নেই।
mone nei.

annoyed বিরক্ত birɔkto
bad খারাপ kharap
confused বিভ্রান্ত bibhranto
good, fine, OK ভাল bhalo
happy খুশি khushi
strange অদ্ভুত odbhut
tired ক্লান্ত klanto

cold ঠাণ্ডা ṭhanḍa
hot গরম gɔrom

PROBLEMS

General Phrases

Is there a problem?
অসুবিধা আছে?
ɔshubidha ache?

No problem.
অসুবিধা নেই।
ɔshubidha nei.

I have a problem.
আমার একটা সমস্যা আছে।
amar ækṭa shɔmossha ache.

What happened?
কি হয়েছে?
ki hoyeche?

Sorry.
দুঃখিত।
dukhito.

Forgive me. / Excuse me.
মাফ করুন।
maph korun.

Please don't touch me.
আমাকে ধরবেন না।
amake dhorben na.

It doesn't matter.
কিছু হবে না।
kichu hɔbe na.

Just a minute.
এক মিনিট।
ek miniṭ.

Hang on a minute.
দেখি একটু।
dekhi ekṭu.

I am not at all happy about this.
এতে আমি মোটেই খুশি নই।
ete ami moṭei khushi noi.

What should I do now?
এখন কি করব?
ekhon ki korbo?

I am very sorry.
আমি খুব দুঃখিত।
ami khub duhkito.

Don't be angry.
রাগ করবেন না।
rag korben na.

Did I say something wrong?
আমি কি খারাপ কিছু বলেছি?
ami ki kharap kichu bolechi?

I made a mistake.
আমার ভুল হয়েছে।
amar bhul hoyeche.

I didn't mean to offend anyone.
আমি কাউকে অপমান করতে চাইনি।
ami kauke ɔpoman korte cai ni.

How can you say that?
আপনি কি করে এ কথা বলতে পারেন।
apni ki kore e kɔtha bolte paren?

No, that's not true at all.
না, না, এটা মোটেই ঠিক নয়।
na, na, eṭa moṭei ṭhik nɔy.

Please don't talk to me like that.
আমার সঙ্গে এইভাবে কথা বলবেন না।
amar shɔngge eibhabe kɔtha bolben na.

SECURITY

Can you help me?
আমাকে সাহায্য করতে পারেন?
amake shahajjo korte paren?

Is there a night-guard here?
এখানে কি দারোয়ান আছে?
ekhane ki darowan achhe?

Can I go there at night?
আমি কি রাত্রে ওখানে যেতে পারি?
ami ki ratre okhane jete pari?

Will someone go with me?
কেউ আমার সঙ্গে যাবে?
keu amar sɔngge jabe?

Where should I put my things/money/passport?
আমার জিনিস-পত্র /টাকা/পাসপোর্ট কোথায় রাখব?
amar jinishpɔtro/ṭaka/pasporṭ kothay rakhbo?

Can I go by myself?
আমি একা যেতে পারি?
ami æka jete pari?

Will you show me the way?
রাস্তাটা আমাকে দেখাবেন?
rastaṭa amake dekhaben?

Will you look after my things for a while?
আপনি আমার জিনিসগুলো একটু দেখবেন?
apni amar jinishgulo ekṭu dekhben?

Don't worry!
চিন্তা করবেন না!
chinta korben na!

There is no danger here.
এখানে কোনও বিপদ নেই।
ekhane kono bipɔd nei.

Careful!
সাবধান!
shabdhan!

Help!
বাঁচান!
bãcan!

Don't go there at night.
ওখানে রাত্রে যাবেন না।
okhane ratre jaben na.

Where are you taking me?
আমাকে কোথায় নিয়ে যাচ্ছেন?
amake kothay niye jacchen?

I don't take drugs.
আমি কোনও নেশা জিনিস খাই না।
ami kono nesha jinish khai na.

Is it safe for me to go on the night bus?
নাইট কোচে যাওয়া আমার পক্ষে ঠিক আছে তো?
naiṭ koce jaowa amar pɔkkhe ṭhi:k ache to?

danger বিপদ bipɔd
safety/security নিরাপত্তা nirapɔtta

SPECIFIC PROBLEMS

I am not well.
আমার শরীর খারাপ।
amar shorir kharap.

I am feeling very ill.
আমার খুব খারাপ লাগছে।
amar khub kharap lagche.

We are having a problem with our car.
আমাদের গাড়ির সমস্যা।
amader gaṛir shɔmossha.

My money has been stolen.
আমার টাকা চুরি হয়েছে।
amar ṭaka curi hoyeche.

I have lost my bag.
আমার ব্যাগ হারিয়ে গেছে।
amar bæg hariye geche.

I don't know this area.
আমি এই এলাকা চিনি না।
ami ei elaka cini na.

I can't wait any longer.
আমি আর দেরি করতে পারছি না।
ami ar deri korte parchi na.

I feel very frightened.
আমার খুব ভয় লাগছে।
amar khub bhɔy lagche.

Has anyone got a cell phone?
কারও মোবাইল আছে?
karo mobail ache?

That is against my religion.
এটা আমার ধর্মের বিরুদ্ধে।
eṭa amar dhɔrmer biruddhe.

Give me some water, please.
আমাকে কিছু পানি দেন।
amake kichu pani den.

Please give me some space.
দয়া করে একটু জায়গা দেন।
dɔya kore ekṭu jayga den.

BEGGING

The general advice is: don't give money! Children begging in the street do not operate on their own and any money they receive will be taken from them and redistributed. Give them something to eat instead which they can consume there and then. When traveling around Dhaka or Kolkata it is a good idea to have a couple of packets of biscuits or some bread with you that you can give out. Those who are not interested in food are not hungry.

These are the phrases you will hear:

বকশিশ
bokshish
baksheesh

গরিব মানুষ
gorib manush
poor person

খানা খাব।
kana khabo.
I will eat.

খিদা লাগছে।
khida lagche.
I am hungry.

পেটে কিছু নেই।
peṭe kichu nei.
There is nothing in my stomach.

দেননা!
denna!
Give!

And here are some responses:

I don't give baksheesh.
আমি বকশিশ দেই না।
ami bokshish dei na.

Excuse me. / Forgive me.
মাফ করেন maph koren
মাফ করুন maph korun

No, I won't give anything.
না, আমি দেব না।
na ami debo na.

Please go away.
দয়া করে চলে যান।
dɔya kore cole jan.

Here you are.
এই যে।
ei je.

God be with you.
আল্লাহ্ হাফেজ।
allah haphez.

In No Uncertain Terms

It is never a good idea to be rude in a foreign language, but sometimes it is necessary to state things clearly and make yourself understood. These are the phrases you may want to use.

Please leave me alone.
দয়া করে আমাকে ছেড়ে দেন।
dɔya kore amake chеṛe den.

Can you please go away?
আপনি চলে যান?
apni cole jan?

I have nothing to say to you.
আপনার সঙ্গে আমার কোনও কথা নেই।
apnar sɔngge amar kono kɔtha nei.

Don't bother me anymore.
আমাকে আর জ্বালাবেন না।
amake ar jalaben na.

I have no intention of coming with you.
আপনার সঙ্গে যাওয়ার আমার কোনও ইচ্ছা নেই।
apnar sɔngge jawar amar kono iccha nei.

What are you looking at?
কি দেখছেন?
ki dekhchen?

That is none of your business.
এটা মোটেই আপনার ব্যাপার নয়।
eṭa moṭei apnar bæpar nɔy.

Don't you have anything else to do?
আপনার কি অন্য কোনও কাজ নেই?
apnar ki ɔnno kono kaj nei?

No thank you, I don't want this.
না, আমি এটা চাই না।
na, ami eṭa cai na.

Don't you understand what 'no' means?
না মানে কি বোঝেন না?
na mane ki bojhen na?

How many more times?
আর কতবার?
ar kɔtobar?

Go away!
চলে যান!
cole jan!

HEALTH AND BODY

HYGIENE

Is this boiled water?
এটা কি ফুটানো পানি?
eṭa ki phuṭano pani?

Can I drink this water?
আমি কি এই পানি খেতে পারি?
ami ki ei pani khete pari?

> **This water is quite OK.**
> এই পানি খেলে কিছু হবে না।
> ei pani khele kichhu hobe na.

Where can I wash my hands?
হাত ধুব কোথায়?
hat dhubo kothay?

Is there any soap?
সাবান আছে?
shaban ache?

The plates are not very clean.
থালাগুলো বেশি পরিষ্কার নয়।
thalagulo beshi porishkar nɔy.

I can't eat/drink that.
আমি এটা খেতে পারি না।
ami eṭa khete pari na.

clean পরিষ্কার porishkar
dirty ময়লা mɔyla

FEELING UNWELL

Call an ambulance, please.
একটা এ্যামবুলেন্স ডাক দেন।
ekṭa æmbulens ḍak den.

I need to see a doctor.
আমাকে ডাক্তারের কাছে যেতে হবে।
amake ḍaktarer kache jete hɔbe.

I had an accident.
আমার একসিডেন্ট হয়েছে।
amar eksiḍenṭ hoyeche.

What happened to you?
আপনার কি হয়েছে?
apnar ki hoyeche?

> **I had a fall.**
> আমি পড়ে গেছি।
> ami poṛe gechi.

Can I sit down somewhere?
কোথাও বসতে পারি?
kothao boshte pari?

I am feeling hot/weak/hungry/tired.
আমার গরম / দুর্বল / খিদা /ক্লান্ত লাগছে।
amar gɔrom/durbol/khida/klanto lagche.

I am (he/she is) ill.
আমার (তার) শরীর খারাপ।
amar (tar) shorir kharap.

I am feeling sick.
আমার বমি হচ্ছে।
amar bomi hocche.

I have a headache.
আমার মাথা ধরেছে।
amar matha dhoreche.

I can't move.
আমি নড়তে পারি না।
ami norte pari na.

I am having problems breathing.
আমার নিঃশ্বাস নিতে কষ্ট হচ্ছে।
amar nisshash nite kɔshṭo hocche.

I am in great pain.
আমার খুব ব্যথা লাগে।
amar khub bætha lage.

I am feeling dizzy.
আমার মাথা ঘুরছে।
amar matha ghurche.

I have a fever.
আমার জ্বর হয়েছে।
amar jɔr hoyeche.

I have been throwing up.
বমি হয়েছে।
bomi hoyeche.

Where is there a toilet here?
টয়লেট এখানে কোথায়।
ṭɔylet ekhane kothay?

Can you show me?
আমাকে দেখাবেন?
amake dækhaben?

Can you take me?
আমাকে নিয়ে যেতে পারেন?
amake niye jete paren?

It's very hot/cold.
খুব গরম । শীত
khub gɔrom/shit.

I need some water.
একটু পানি দেন।
ekṭu pani den.

I can't sleep.
আমি ঘুমাতে পারি না।
ami ghumate pari na.

You are not pregnant, are you?
আপনার বাচ্চা হবে না তো?
apnar baccha hɔbe na to?

I am (she is) pregnant.
আমার (তার) পেটে বাচ্চা।
amar (tar) peṭe baccha.

I am having an asthma attack.
আমার হাঁপানি হচ্ছে।
amar hapani hocche.

I have diabetes.
আমার ডাইবিটিস আছে।
amar daibitis ache.

I am (he/she is) bleeding.
রক্ত পড়ছে।
rɔkto poṛche.

Can you help me?
আমাকে সাহায্য করতে পারেন?
amake shahajjo korte paren?

Lie down!
আপনি শুয়ে থাকেন!
apni shuye thaken!

Will you stay with me?
আমার সঙ্গে থাকবেন তো?
amar shɔngge thakben to.

I don't need anything else.
আর কোনও কিছুর দরকার নেই।
ar kono kichur dɔrkar nei.

Thank you very much.
আপনাকে অনেক ধন্যবাদ।
apnake ɔnek dhɔnnobad.

I am feeling a bit better now.
এখন একটু ভাল লাগছে।
ækhon ekṭu bhalo lagche.

Parts of the Body and Illnesses

back পিঠ piṭh
blood রক্ত rɔkto
body গা ga, শরীর shorir
breast / chest বুক buk
breath নিঃশ্বাস nisshash
cold, flu সর্দি shordi
cough কাশি kashi
diarrhea / dysentry আমাশা amasha
doctor ডাক্তার ḍaktar
ear কান kan
examine পরীক্ষা করা porikkha kɔra
eye চোখ cokh
face / mouth মুখ mukh
fever জ্বর jɔr
finger / toe আঙুল anggul
foot / leg পা pa
hair চুল cul
hand / arm হাত hat
head মাথা matha
health স্বাস্থ্য shastho, শরীর shorir
heart হৃদয় ridɔy
hip পাছা pacha
ill অসুস্থ ɔsustho

illness অসুখ ɔsukh
infection সংক্রমণ shɔngkromon
lungs ফুসফুস phushphush
medicine ওসুধ oshudh
neck ঘাড় ghaṛ
nose নাক nak
nurse সেবিকা shebika
pain ব্যথা bætha
pregnant গর্ভবতী gɔrbhoboti
skin চামড়া camṛa
spine মেরুদণ্ড merudɔnḍo
stomach পেট peṭ
throat গলা gɔla
tongue জিভ jibh
tooth দাঁত dãt
treatment চিকিৎসা cikitsha
vaccination টিকা ṭika
waist / midriff কোমর komor

WEATHER AND NATURE

TALKING ABOUT THE WEATHER

What a beautiful day.
কি সুন্দর দিন!
ki shundor din!

a lovely breeze
খুব সুন্দর বাতাস।
khub shundor batash.

It will be a very hot day.
দিনটা খুব গরম হবে।
dinṭa khub gɔrom hɔbe.

It won't be very hot today.
আজকে বেশি গরম হবে না।
ajke beshi gɔrom hɔbe na.

Will it rain today?
আজ কি বৃষ্টি হবে?
aj ki brishṭi hɔbe?

> **Yes, there is heavy rain coming.**
> হ্যাঁ, বড় বৃষ্টি আসছে।
> hæ̃, boṛo brishṭi ashche.

When will it stop raining?
বৃষ্টি কোন সময় থামবে?
brishṭi kon shɔmɔy thambe?

If the rain doesn't stop, the road will get flooded.
বৃষ্টি না থামলে রাস্তায় পানি উঠবে।
brishṭi na thamle, rastay pani uṭhbe.

There are lots of clouds in the sky.
আকাশে অনেক মেঘ।
akashe ɔnek megh.

There may be a storm.
ঝড় হতে পারে।
jhoṛ hote pare.

It will get cold tonight.
রাত্রে শীত পড়বে।
ratre shit poṛbe.

It's very foggy today.
আজকে খুব কুয়াশা।
ajke khub kuwasha.

Don't sit in the sun.
রোদে বসবেন না
rode boshben na.

There is no shade anywhere.
একটুও ছায়া নেই কোথাও
ekṭuo chaya nei kothao.

NATURE WORDS

air / wind হাওয়া haowa, বাতাস batash
cloud মেঘ megh
cold শীত shit
darkness অন্ধকার ɔndhokar
death মৃত্যু mritu
desert মরুভূমি morubhumi
drought অনাবৃষ্টি ɔnabrishti
dust ধুলা dhula
earth / soil মাটি maṭi
fire আগুন agun
flood বন্যা bɔnna
fog কুয়াশা kuwasha
forest বন bon
full moon পূর্ণিমা purnima
grass ঘাস ghash
heat গরম gɔrom
hurricane ঘূর্ণিঝড় ghurnijhɔṛ

ice / snow বরফ bɔroph
land জমি jomi
light আলো alo
lightning বিজলি bijoli
life জীবন jibon
monsoon বর্ষা bɔrsha
moon চাঁদ cãd
mountain পাহাড় pahaṛ
nature প্রকৃতি prokriti
ocean /sea সাগর shagor, সমুদ্র shomudro
plant চারা cara
rain বৃষ্টি brishṭi
river নদী nodi
riverbank পাড় paṛ
rock / stone পাথর pathor
sand বালু balu
sea / ocean সাগর shagor, সমুদ্র shomudro
season কাল kal, ঋতু ritu
shade ছায়া chaya
sky আকাশ akash
snow / ice বরফ bɔroph
stars তারা tara
stone / rock পাথর pathor
storm ঝড় jhɔṛ
sun সূর্য shurjo
sunrise সূর্যোদয় shurjodɔy
sunset সূর্যাস্ত shurjasto
sunshine রোদ rod
thunder মেঘের ডাক megher ḍak
tornado / cyclone ঘূর্ণিঝড় ghurnijhɔr
tree গাছ gach
universe বিশ্ব bissho
water জল jɔl, পানি pani
wave ঢেউ ḍheu
weather আবহাওয়া abhaowa
world পৃথিবী prithibi, দুনিয়া duniya

PLANTS AND CROPS

bamboo বাঁশ bãsh
banyan tree বট গাছ bɔṭ gach
betel পান pan
branch ডাল ḍal
cane বেত bet
china rose জবা jɔba
cotton তুলা tula
creeper লতা lɔta
flower ফুল phu:l
jute পাট pa:ṭ
leaf পাতা pata
lotus / water-lily পদ্ম pɔddo
mangrove গরান gɔran
palm tree তাল গাছ ta:l ga:ch
rice (paddy) ধান dha:n
root শিকড় shikoṛ
rose গোলাপ golap
sandal চন্দন cɔndon
silk রেশম reshom
tobacco তামাক tamak
tree গাছ ga:ch
tuberose রজনিগন্ধা rɔjonighɔndha
water-lily / lotus পদ্ম pɔddo
wheat গম gɔm

TIME, DAYS, MONTHS, SEASONS

TELLING THE TIME

What time is it?
কয়টা বাজে?
kɔyṭa baje?

(At) what time?
কোন সময়?
kon shɔmɔy?

For how long?
কতক্ষণ?
kɔtokkhɔn?

one o'clock	**two o'clock**	**three o'clock**
একটা ækṭa	দুইটা duiṭa	তিনটা বাজে tinṭa baje

half past সাড়ে shaṛe

half past one	**half past two**	**half past three**
দেড়টা	আড়াইটা	সাড়ে তিনটা
deṛta	aṛaiṭa	shaṛe tinṭa

quarter past সওয়া shɔowa

quarter past nine
সওয়া নয়টা
shɔowa nɔyṭa

quarter to পৌনে poune

quarter to twelve
পৌনে বারোটা
poune baroṭa

one hour	**two hours**	**three hours**
এক æk ghɔnṭa	দুই dui ghɔnṭa	তিন ঘণ্টা tin ghɔnṭa

before / earlier আগে age
later পরে pɔre

an hour ago এক ঘণ্টা আগে æk ghɔnṭa age
in an hour এক ঘণ্টা পরে æk ghɔnṭa pɔre
half an hour আধা ঘণ্টা adha ghɔnṭa
four forty = twenty to five চারটা চল্লিশ carṭa collish
ten past one একটা দশ ækṭa dɔsh

Times of the Day

afternoon বিকাল bikal
dawn ভোর bhor
day দিন din
evening সন্ধ্যা sɔndha
midday দুপুর dupur
morning সকাল shɔkal
night রাত rat

Days of the Week

Sunday রবিবার robibar
Monday সোমবার shombar
Tuesday মঙ্গলবার mɔnggolbar
Wednesday বুধবার budhbar
Thursday বৃহস্পতিবার brihoshpotibar
Friday শুক্রবার shukrobar
Saturday শনিবার shonibar

Months and Seasons

The Bengali calendar is still in use with monolingual publishers and newspapers. The Bengali new century, 1400, began on April, 15, 1993. The second half of the year 2010 is therefore 1417 on the Bengali calendar. Bengalis count six seasons, lasting two months each.

Months

April – May বৈশাখ boishakh
May – June জ্যৈষ্ঠ joishṭho
June –July আষাঢ় ashaṛh
July – August শ্রাবণ sraboṇ
August – September ভাদ্র bhadro
September – October আশ্বিন ashin
October – November কার্তিক kartik
November – December অগ্রহায়ণ ɔgrohayon
December – January পৌষ pouṣ
January – February মাঘ magh
March – April চৈত্র coitro

Seasons

summer (April – June) গ্রীষ্ম grissho
rainy season (June – August) বর্ষা bɔrsha
early autumn (August – October) শরৎ śɔrot
late autumn (October – December) হেমন্ত hemonto
winter (December – February) শীত shi:t
spring (February – April) বসন্ত bɔshonto

Other Time Words

time সময় shɔmɔy

day দিন din
week সপ্তাহ shɔptaho, সপ্তা shɔpta
month মাস mash
year বছর bɔchor

minute মিনিট miniṭ
hour ঘণ্টা ghɔnṭa

now এখন ekhon
then তখন tɔkhon

today আজ, আজকে aj, ajke
yesterday গতকাল gɔtokal
tomorrow আগামীকাল agamikal

last week গত সপ্তাহ gɔto shɔptaho
last month গত মাস gɔto mash
last year গত বছর gɔto bɔchor

next week আগামী সপ্তা agami shɔptaho
next month আগামী মাস agami mash
next year আগামী বছর agami bɔchor

before, earlier আগে age
after, later পরে pɔre

early সকালে shɔkale
late দেরিতে derite

at first প্রথমে prothome
in the beginning / at first শুরুতে shurute
in the end শেষে sheshe

always সব সময় shɔb shɔmɔy
all day long সারা দিন shara din
never কখনও না kɔkhono na

COLORS

black কালো kalo
blue নীল ni:l
brown বাদামি badami
gold সোনার sonar
green সবুজ shobuj
grey ছাই রং chai rɔng
orange কমলা kɔmla
pink গোলাপি golapi
purple বেগুনি beguni
red লাল la:l
silver রূপার rupa
white সাদা shada
yellow হলদে hɔlde, হলুদ holud

AMOUNTS

all সব shɔb
any কোনও kono
at least অন্তত ɔntoto
every প্রতি proti
how much কত kɔto
less কম kɔm
a little অল্প ɔlpo, একটু ekṭu
a lot / many অনেক ɔnek
more আর ar, আরও aro
nothing কিছু না kichu na
only মাত্র, শুধু matro, shudhu
some কিছু kichu
so much এত æto
such এমন æmon
too much / too many বেশি beshi
very খুব khub
the whole of সমস্ত shɔmosto

PEOPLE

GENERAL

actor নায়ক nayok
actress নায়িকা nayika
artist শিল্পী shilpi
ayah আয়া ayah
barber নাপিত napit
beggar ভিক্ষুক bhikkhuk
boy ছেলে chele
brother (*older*) দাদা dada; (*younger*) ভাই bhai
carpenter মিস্ত্রি mistri
child বাচ্চা bacchha, শিশু shishu
clergyman / pastor যাজক jajok (*m*) যাজিকা jajika (*f*)
cook বাবুর্চি baburci
daughter মেয়ে meye
doctor ডাক্তার ḍaktar
dressmaker / tailor দর্জি dorji
driver চালক chalok
farmer কৃষক krishok
father বাবা baba, অব্বা abba
father-in-law শ্বশুর shoshur
friend (*female*) বান্ধবি bandhobi; (*male*) বন্ধু bondhu
girl মেয়ে meye
guard / gate-keeper দারোয়ান darowan
human being মানুষ manush
husband স্বামী shami
journalist সাংবাদিক shangbadik
landlord বাড়িওয়ালা bariowala
lawyer উকিল ukil
man পুরুষ purush
mother মা ma, অম্মা amma
mother-in-law শাশুড়ি shashuṛi
nurse নার্স nars, সেবক shebok (*m*), সেবিকা shebika (*f*)
parents মা–বাবা ma–baba

people / person লোক lok
poet কবি kobi
politician রাজনীতিক rajnitik
prime minister প্রধানমন্ত্রী prodhan montri
rickshaw-driver রিকশাওয়ালা rikshaowala
servant কাজের লোক kajer lok, চাকর cakor
shopkeeper দোকান্দার dokandar
sister (*older*) দিদি didi, আপা apa; (*younger*) বোন bon
social worker সমাজসেবী shɔmajshebi
son ছেলে chele
student ছাত্র chatro (*m*), ছাত্রী chatri (*f*)
tailor / dressmaker দর্জি dorji
teacher শিক্ষক shikkhok (*m*) শিক্ষিকা shikkhika (*f*)
traveler যাত্রী jatri
wife স্ত্রী stri, বউ bou
woman মহিলা mohila

KINSHIP TERMS

Bengalis are very precise in the naming of their relatives. An aunt can be your mother's sister, your father's sister, your mother's brother's wife, or your father's brother's wife and they are all addressed differently. Muslims and Hindus tend to use different terminology. Here are the important terms. They are not in alphabetical order.

(*first term is Muslim; second is Hindu*)

younger brother ভাই bhai; ভাই bhai
older brother বড় ভাই bɔṛo bhai; দাদা dada

younger sister বোন bon; বোন bon
older sister আপা apa; দিদি didi

grandson নাতি nati; নাতি nati
granddaughter নাতনি natni; নাতনি natni

In-laws

These terms are the same for Muslims and Hindus. They are generally not used in addressing people.

husband স্বামী shami
wife স্ত্রী stri, বউ bou

father-in-law শ্বশুর shoshur
mother-in-law শাশুড়ি shashuṛi

daughter's husband জামাই jamai
son's wife বউ bou

older sister's husband দুলাভাই dulabhai

older brother's wife বউদি boudi *or* ভাবী bhabi
younger brother's wife বউমা bouma

wife's older brother সম্বন্ধী shɔmmondhi
wife's younger brother শালা shala

wife's younger sister শালি shali

husband's older brother ভাশুর bhashur
husband's younger brother দেবর debor

husband's older sister ননাস nɔnash
husband's younger sister ননদ nɔnod

Paternal relatives

(*first term is Muslim; second is Hindu*)

father আব্বা abba; বাবা baba
grandfather দাদা dada; ঠাকুরদা ṭhakurda
grandmother দাদি dadi; ঠাকুরমা ṭhakurma
father's older brother বড় চাচা bɔṛo; জেঠা jeṭha caca
father's older brother's wife বড় চাচি bɔṛo caci; জেঠি jeṭhi
father's younger brother চাচা caca; কাকা kaka
father's younger brother's wife চাচি caci; কাকি kaki
father's sister ফুফু phuphu; পিসি pishi

father's sister's husband ফুফা phupha; পিসা pisha
brother's son (nephew) ভাতিজা bhatija; ভাইস্তা bhaista
brother's daughter (niece) ভাতিজি bhatiji; ভাইস্তি bhaisti

Maternal relatives

(*first term is Muslim; second is Hindu*)

mother আম্মা amma; মা ma
grandfather নানা nana; দাদু dadu
grandmother নানি nani; দিদিমা didima
mother's brother মামা mama; মামা mama
mother's brother's wife মামি mami; মামি mami
mother's sister খালা khala; মাসি mashi
mother's sister's husband খালু khalu; মেসো mesho
sister's son (nephew) ভাগনে bhagne; ভাগনে bhagne
sister's daughter (niece) ভাগ্নি bhagni; ভাগ্নি bhagni

ANIMALS, BIRDS, INSECTS

animal পশু poshu, জীবজন্তু jibjontu
ant পিঁপড়া pĩpṛa
bat বাদুড় baduṛ
bee মৌমাছি moumachi
bird পাখি pakhi
buffalo মহিষ mohish
bug ছারপোকা charpoka
bull / ox ষাঁড় shãṛ
butterfly প্রজাপতি projapoti
calf বাছুর bachur
camel উট uṭ
cat বেড়াল, বিড়াল beṛal, biṛal
cattle গরু goru
chicken মুরগি murgi
cock মোরগ morog
cockroach তেলাপোকা telapoka
cow গরু goru
crocodile কুমির kumir
crow কাক ka:k
cuckoo কোকিল kokil
deer হরিণ horin
dog কুকুর kukur
donkey গাধা gadha
dove ঘুঘু ghughu
duck হাঁস hãsh
eagle ঈগল i:gol
elephant হাতি hati
firefly জোনাকি jonaki
fish মাছ ma:ch
fly মাছি machi
fox jackal শিয়াল shiyal
frog ব্যাং bæng
goat ছাগল chagol
goose / swan রাজহাঁস rajhãsh

horse ঘোড়া ghoṛa
insect পোকা poka
lamb / sheep ভেড়া bhæṛa
leopard চিতা cita
lion সিংহ shingho
monkey বানর banor
mosquito মশা mɔsha
mouse ইঁদুর ĩdur
parrot টিয়া পাখি ṭiya pakhi
peacock ময়ূর moyur
pig শূকর shukor
pigeon কবুতর kobutor
prawn চিংড়ি মাছ cingṛi ma:ch
rabbit খরগোশ khɔrgosh
sheep / lamb ভেড়া bhæṛa
snake সাপ sha:p
sparrow চড়াই cɔṛai
spider মাকড়সা makoṛsha
squirrel কাঠ বিড়ালি kaṭh biṛali
swan / goose রাজহাঁস rajhãsh
tiger বাঘ ba:gh
vulture শকুনি shokuni
whale তিমি timi

NUMBERS

Bangla numbers are not easy to learn as there is no automatic repetitive succession in the tens, such as *twenty-two, thirty-two, forty-two* in English. English numbers are, however, readily understood. Here are just a few useful numbers to know.

one এক æk
two দুই dui
three তিন tin
four চার car
five পাঁচ pãc
six ছয় chɔy
seven সাত shat
eight আট aṭ
nine নয় nɔy
ten দশ dosh
eleven এগার ægaro
twelve বার baro
thirteen তের tero
fourteen চৌদ্দ couddo
fifteen পনের pɔnero
sixteen ষোল sholo
seventeen সতের shɔtero
eighteen আঠার aṭharo
nineteen উনিশ unish
twenty বিশ bish
twenty-one একুশ ekush
twenty-two বাইশ baish
twenty-three তেইশ teish
twenty-four চব্বিশ cobbish
twenty-five পঁচিশ põcish
twenty-six ছাব্বিশ chabbish
twenty-seven সাতাশ satash; সাতাইশ sataish
twenty-eight আটাশ aṭash; আটাইশ aṭaish

twenty-nine উনত্রিশ unôtriś
thirty ত্রিশ trish
forty চল্লিশ collish
fifty পঞ্চাশ pɔncash
sixty ষাট shaṭ
seventy সত্তর shottor
eighty আশি ashi
ninety নব্বই nɔbboi
one hundred একশ æk sho
two hundred দুশ du sho
one thousand এক হাজার æk hajar
one hundred thousand এক লাখ æk lakh
ten million এক কোটি æk koṭi
zero শূন্য shunno
one and a half দেড় deṛ
two and a half আড়াই aṛai